THE URBANA FREE LIBRARY
D0987646

PUSHKIN P

MEMOR
OF
LOW
TIDE

‘A story of inheritance, of the fluidity of a mother–daughter relationship dissolved in a calm sea, a kind of reverse amniotic fluid in which to dive and luxuriate deliciously’

Marie Claire

‘This is an infinitely gentle, oblique look at a whole century, passed through as a swimmer crosses the water, from one buoy to another… Haunting and elegiac’

Livres Hebdo

‘As you turn these dazzling pages, you pass from levity to humour, from insouciance to nostalgia, from necessary frivolity to deep solemnity’

Le Figaro

‘[C … ary genre:
th … ohy’

L’Obs

DISCARDED BY THE URBANA FREE LIBRARY
The Urbana Free Library
To renew: call **217-367-4057**
or go to **urbanafreelibrary.org**
and select **My Account**

CHANTAL THOMAS was raised at the seaside in Arcachon, near Bordeaux. She has taught literature in a number of American universities and is the author of over 20 books. She also works as a screenwriter. She won the Prix Femina for her novel *Farewell My Queen* (2002), also adapted as a film by Benoit Jacquot, and later received the prestigious Roger-Caillois and Prince de Monaco prizes for her entire work.

NATASHA LEHRER is a translator, literary editor and writer. Her co-translation of *Suite for Barbara Loden*, by Nathalie Léger, won the 2017 Scott Moncrieff translation prize. She lives in Paris.

MEMORIES OF LOW TIDE

CHANTAL THOMAS

TRANSLATED FROM THE FRENCH
BY NATASHA LEHRER

PUSHKIN PRESS

Pushkin Press
71–75 Shelton Street
London WC2H 9JQ

Original text © Chantal Thomas 2017
English translation © Natasha Lehrer 2019
Copyright © Editions du Seuil 2017

Memories of Low Tide was first published as *Souvenirs de la marée basse* in France, 2017

First published by Pushkin Press in 2019.
This edition published in 2020.

This book is supported by the Institut français (Royaume-Uni) as part of the Burgess programme.

INSTITUT FRANÇAIS
ROYAUME-UNI

9 8 7 6 5 4 3 2 1

ISBN 13: 978-1-78227-520-6

All rights reserved. No part of this publication may be reproduced, stored in a retrieval system or transmitted in any form or by any means, electronic, mechanical, photocopying, recording or otherwise, without prior permission in writing from Pushkin Press

Epigraph Colette, *Belles saisons* © Flammarion, 1955

Quotation on page 10 from *Sade, Fourier, Loyola* by Roland Barthes, translated by Richard Miller (University of California Press: Berkeley and Los Angeles, 1989)

Extracts on pages 82–4 from *Bains de Mer* © Heir of Paul Morand, 2019

Quotation on page 101 from *The Way by Swann's* by Marcel Proust, translated by Lydia Davis (Allen Lane, The Penguin Press, 2002)

Extracts on pages 224–5 from François Mauriac, *Journal d'un homme de 30 ans* © Flammarion

Designed and typeset by Tetragon, London
Printed and bound by CPI Group (UK) Ltd, Croydon, CR0 4YY

www.pushkinpress.com

FOR THIERRY

L'ENFANT VEUT UNE VAGUE SALÉE, LE SABLE.

THE CHILD WANTS A SALTY WAVE, THE SAND.

COLETTE

BEGINNING

This morning I woke up to dark clouds in the sky, after two months without rain. I didn't need to go outside to find out. I could see from my bed the palm trees swaying in the wind in the eerie, leaden light, their brilliant green fronds shrouded in grey. I'd slept a long time, without the usual interruptions occasioned by the light as it grew brighter, the daily miracle of a new day heralded by the gulls' shrieks and the doves' low cooing. Here in Nice, during the summer months, I wake up in several stages. This is not because I'm anxious; on the contrary, it's because I'm impatient for the light, the *nuances* of the light, that my sleep is unsettled. Long before the sun is fully up the light is greenish white, becoming slowly tinged with pink, before it finally blooms – and this is what wakes me properly – into the pure gleam of clear gold.

The summer is blazing hot. Everything burns to the touch. It's exhilarating and exhausting all at once. As if we were on the brink of some extraordinary event: catastrophe or revelation. There's urgency in the air: to explode, go wild, add the fever of alcohol to that of the world, turn up the music full blast, sit alone on a rock, laughing, legs in the water, watching the sun set. And when the foehn, the hot wind from the mountains to the south, begins to rise in repeated gusts, it feels like the Event is imminent. Waves surge, temperatures soar, and along the pavement little piles of pine needles and dried leaves blown from inland are trampled underfoot.

Today's not like that at all. The sky is overcast, wind laced with rain. I gulp down my coffee and grab a towel, flip-flops for walking on the pebbles and a canvas sun hat, in the unlikely event that the sun should return, shove it all into my multi-coloured Brazilian beach bag and hurry down towards the sea. It's dark and furious, nothing like the Mediterranean that I swam in the previous evening. A calm sea, shimmering with coppery glints, like moiré silk. An enveloping sea, whose balmy embrace made me feel like I was swimming in a dream. Why would I ever stop, I asked myself, as in the dusk a buoy blinked its green light and the street lamps along the coast came on. When I got home I flicked randomly through a book by Roland Barthes and came across a paragraph on Sade: "The ultimate erotic state (analogous to the sublime legato of the phrase, which in music is called *phrasing*) is to swim: in corporeal substances, delights, the deep feelings of lasciviousness."

Because of the sudden bad weather, I am instinctively careful not to swim against the waves but to plunge down with them and let them bring me back up, closing my eyes against the foaming crests as they smack me in the face. It's beginning to pour, huge drops scoring the water. It's pure joy to be swimming in both sea and rain at once, the rain falling in sheets, drenching my head. But it's such a deluge in the lashing waves that I can no longer see, and I get out, a little dazed. My clothes and towel are soaked. My bag is full of water. There's no point trying to find shelter so I go up to the boardwalk, where enormous masses of water are crashing with astonishing force. On the ground they create rushing rivers, out at sea immense, light-coloured, faintly ruffled areas of water. As the storm becomes more intense these zones grow bigger, as if the rain bouncing on the sea was sufficiently forceful and abundant to replace the surface of the sea with a surface of fresh water, fleetingly obliterating it. I'm struck by how the power of the sea's erasure and perpetual renewal is exceeded by that of the rain. The sea, streaked with rain, swept clear of the slanting lines of waves, extends all the way to the Restaurant La Réserve, reaching another buoy and stretching out towards the horizon.

My mother used sometimes to come here to swim, although her regular beach was near where she lived at the end of the Promenade des Anglais, in front of the Hotel Westminster. But she also swam opposite the Cours Saleya. She didn't really have a regular beach, in fact. Even towards the end of her life, at an age when the normal tendency is to reduce physical effort, she would often take the train to Villefranche-sur-Mer, where she liked to swim in the bay – she preferred its size and claimed it was more sheltered than the Bay of Angels. She would swim anywhere, at all times of the day, with a stubbornness and tenacity that she didn't display towards any other activity.

Still in my swimming costume, standing above the waves and clutching my dripping clothes, I abandon myself to the torrential rain. Water from the sky streams down my face and into my eyes, is seasoned with the salt from my own body. I've always thought of my mother as a woman who was entirely indifferent to any notion of transmission, and myself as someone who had appeared out of nowhere, with no anterior wisdom, yet suddenly it seems to me that she has, without knowing it, transmitted something truly essential to me: the energy of the wake as it carves through the water, imprinted in the moment; the beauty of a path that leads to forgetting; and if there was something I wanted to celebrate about her, something of her that I wanted to try to convey, it would be, paradoxically, the figure of a woman who forgets. Not who is indifferent, but who forgets. Was this her strength or her weakness? Both, surely; and as I stand in the pouring rain, soaked in the deluge, my beach things about to be carried away by the current, borne off by a swollen wave, I find myself wishing I were already home, lost in the music of writing, watching the curtain of rain, looking through it at something far beyond, my mother swimming, alone, unreachable, a minuscule speck against the blue immensity, an almost imperceptible dot, except in my own memory.

NICE, AUGUST 2015

I
ARCACHON TIME

DREAM

I am standing at the top of a dune. Below me: the sea, green, astonishingly clear, limpid as oyster water. There are zones of deeper green, whose forms follow the sand's undulations, shifting according to the shapes of the shadows that trace the different accumulations of sand at the bottom of the Arcachon Bay. I first catch sight of this magnificent, irresistible body of water through the dark, slightly warped, curving silhouettes of the pine trees. The landscape is vast. It seems to me that everything – the green sea, the height of the dune, the pine trees – is so much larger than nature. A perfectly frontal image. An image that says to me: Look at what's there, right in front of your eyes.

In the same dream (but now I'm in Arcachon on the Eyrac jetty, standing next to a carousel that has been going round and round forever), I proclaim: "The most beautiful place is the place where I live." Stowed within that sentence is the image of the walk along the beach between the jetty and the alleyway at the end of the road that I took as a child when I went down to swim.

THE SWIMMER OF THE GRAND CANAL

Whenever my grandmother Eugénie used to talk about my mother as a young girl, she would tell the same two stories. First, how Jackie, who was obsessed with exercise, would always find a way to set up some corner of her workplace dedicated to her passion: once she fixed parallel bars in the back corridor of the lawyer's office where she was briefly employed as a secretary, and when she was working for a notary she used to unroll a bath mat in a corner so she could do her sit-ups. And my grandmother loved to tell the story of that day in the middle of July when her daughter was overcome by a mad impulse to leap into the Grand Canal in the gardens of Versailles and swim, calmly, in her elegant, superbly cadenced crawl, fast but not too fast; her steady crawl which made her seem, to anyone watching her at work in the water, like a force that could keep going forever. But that particular day it was unlikely that she'd be allowed to keep going for very long...

Among all the characters whom I've pictured at the Palace of Versailles and its gardens in the course of my walks and my readings – alongside the remarkable Duchess of Burgundy, on hot summer nights, lifting her skirts with both hands and running barefoot over the green carpet of lawn, the Princess Palatine splitting off at a gallop from a hunting party without warning, the young infanta of Spain, Mariana Victoria, playing hide-and-seek behind the crimson curtains in the Hall of Mirrors, Marie-Antoinette in a fur bonnet, aged fifteen, eagerly awaiting a sleigh race, jumping up and down with excitement – there is my mother. She must have been sixteen or seventeen. Her parents had moved away from Versailles and 15 Rue Sainte-Adélaïde, the house where she was born, not far from the Queen's Gate. She lived with them in Viroflay but she often cycled back through the forest to Versailles. She did not have a specific plan that morning to swim in the Grand Canal, but she always took her bathing suit with her, just in case, and when she arrived, sweating, at the sparkling plane of water where a drowned rowboat foundered, when she saw the empty banks bordered by paths that ran on into the bushes, she was filled with a wondrous sense of freedom. Uniquely sensitive to the charms of these gardens that had been left to go wild, and completely unimpressed by the grandiose architecture of Power radiated by the palace itself, she took off her short-sleeved blouse and her culottes until she was standing in her bathing costume, walked down the steps that disappeared into the water, and dived in. It wasn't so much that what she was doing was forbidden, and that she had to hurry before she was stopped in her tracks. It was more as though she were responding to an invitation to swim from the glimmering water itself. Rules, all rules, fell within the sphere of an order of reality that did not exist for her. In the spinney known as the Ballroom Bosquet, where she took her first steps, in the Orangery, where she used to play in the sun, by the Neptune fountain, where she liked to plunge her dolls' heads under the water, in every corner of the palace gardens, she felt entirely at home. And in the Grand Canal as well.

Jackie was no more concerned by the possible reactions of any guards who might be about than she was by all the objects that have, over the course of the centuries, been either dropped by accident or deliberately thrown into the water, and which now lie at the bottom of the canal. Lockets, snuffboxes, gold coins, wedding rings, hairpins, shoe buckles, inkwells, the remnants of fans which are now nothing but their armatures, silver platters from a hunting dinner cast into the water by some servant weary of the endless cleaning and polishing, religious statuettes gaily tossed away by an impious young nun, a portrait of Madame de Maintenon riddled with pinholes... Trifles, certainly, that could easily go unnoticed by an athletic young woman of the 20th century – but what of the important treasures, like the splendid Venetian gondolas that once belonged to Louis XIV, which now lie sunken and rotting in the silt, the black figures on the prow all that remains, reaching up towards the surface – how was it possible to ignore them? Well, she seemed to manage. Just as she ignored the trembling silhouettes, the formless assemblage of petrified mummies who suddenly began to gather on different floors of the chateau and were pressing up against the windows, astonished at the extraordinary sight of a girl on a bicycle, a girl undressing in the open air and diving into the water. A girl swimming! Of course, there were those who had already seen a person swimming, indeed, some of them even knew how to swim. Men. For the women, it was clearly out of the question. Well-born women, well-brought-up women, do not swim! What's more there was the complicated and impossibly time-consuming matter of undressing. Swimming! The very idea! What madness! More and more were now gathering by the windows. Men, out of a long-standing, libertine habit. Women, driven by a reflex, purporting to be pious. Burning with indignation. At the same time – I know because one Bastille Day, as an extra in *Farewell, My Queen*, I had to wear the celebrated costume of the court (its dignified appearance offset by the weight of several kilos of velvet, a corset that cuts off your breathing, the incessant trickle of sweat down your back, your armpits, between your breasts and your thighs, muddying your make-up, and, underneath your wig, pins and hair slides tugging at the roots of your hair, digging in and tearing your scalp) – they would have given every last thing they possessed, these women who had nothing left to give, to swap places with that girl who was swimming, to live in a world, even for just an hour, even *en passant*, where they were free to come and go without an escort, allowed to do as they pleased, to do what they wanted. It sometimes seemed to them, during the stagnant eternity of their living death, as they became lost in their reveries, thinking back over their lived existence, that they were nothing more than pedestals for displaying jewellery. It was as if their entire existence could be reduced to a sequence of assembling their coiffure, applying face paint and powder, clothes fittings, being dressed and undressed. Not a word remained, not even the slightest trace of gossip exchanged in front of the mirror as they were at their toilette, obsequious smiles imprinted in clouds of powder. Supererogatory mannequins. Decorative adornments. Did they exist only for their beauty? Absolutely not. Their primary purpose was the perpetuation of a name and hence their duty was to provide sons. They were celebrated for their ornamentation, complimented on their features, but really they were no more than cogs in a programme of reproduction... They were told again and again that water was unsanitary, that they must be wary of it and parsimonious in its use, but that must surely have been a lie told by the men to keep them prisoner. Getting into the water, diving down, coming back up to the surface, floating, drifting... What must it be like, they wondered, their eyes fixed on the gamine young woman, to feel that caress insinuating itself into every part of you, that softness wrapping your back as gently as it strokes your thighs and plays around your lips? They stared out of the hollows of their eye sockets at the slender young girl, the creature moving with such lightness through water and air. Jealousy ravaged what was left of their features.

The swimmer of the Grand Canal revelled in the water, not a care in the world, euphoric with delight. Whatever might exist around, below, above her, she gave no thought to it.

She felt only the deliciousness of the water against her skin, its bracing, invigorating immersion.

I was wrong to say that somebody soon arrived to stop her. It was a time when there was little interest in the Palace of Versailles, few tourists and minimal surveillance, and so she was able to swim up and down the royal canal for a while before an old man noticed her. In the time it took him to hobble over to the water's edge Jackie had already got out, got dressed and got on her bicycle. In the breeze stirred up by its speed, with water saturating her bathing suit and soaking her clothes, she cycled the whole way home in a refreshing mist.

In the long-uninhabited chateau, the crowd of ghosts vanished. They disappeared back into their night. They could not even say what it was that they had seen that troubled them so deeply. In the country of the dead there are no new words. *Bicycle,* such a joyful word, or the sensual *crawl*, do not exist.

FIRST HOLIDAYS

The parents of the swimmer of the Grand Canal lived through a revolution in the routine of their existence: the law of 20th June 1936 decreeing the universal right to paid holidays. With this legislation the Front Populaire brought to an end the centuries-old tradition of a society split in two: a rich and leisured minority and the huge majority, impoverished to varying degrees, yoked to labour from morning to night, from childhood to death – in short, not such a different life from that of the indentured servants of the *ancien régime*. I remember when I was living in a maid's room on the Avenue de la Bourdonnais, the owner of the building, an old man who limped yet who always seemed to be climbing up to his seventh floor, used to roam the corridors, checking that his servants hadn't forgotten that it was time for *their* mass, the one said every day, not just on Sundays, at six in the morning, that was reserved for the domestic servants. He never knocked at my door, but he would slow down in front of it, hear that I was already up and leafing through my various editions of books by the Marquis de Sade, my Pauvert collection bound in black and gold, my Demon missal, busy typing up my ideas about this "macabre individual, the shame of the aristocracy, the scourge of morality and religion", as he once described the Marquis when I went down to his apartment to pay my rent. The Front Populaire couldn't radically change society with this one law, but nonetheless, after 1st July 1936, many French people began to discover the privilege of sleeping in late several days in a row, fourteen to be precise; and, even more remarkable, the landmark experience of leaving town, discovering the mountains for the first time, the astonishment of seeing the sea. My grandmother championed the government's socialist initiatives, particularly because – she was thinking of her daughter – it set up an "Under-Secretariat for Sport and Leisure", immediately branded by the right the "Ministry of Idleness". My grandfather, inclined to idleness himself, avoided political arguments. He was happy just giving thanks to Providence. As he was a graphic illustrator for the SNCF, which qualified him as a *cheminot*, or railway worker, he was entitled to free train tickets, and my grandparents chose delightful holiday destinations. First Lake Como, in Italy, where my grandmother saw her first oleander; the following summer Arcachon, which was to lead to a decisive change in their future and, several years later, in mine.

They chose Arcachon because of its air and specifically its effects on the lungs, because as a result of the

1914–18 war my grandfather suffered from respiratory problems. They left Viroflay with the idea of profiting as much as possible from this blessed fortnight by the sea, two weeks of being paid for doing nothing, discovering the art of *far niente*, of lazing about, not necessarily an innate talent despite its apparent effortlessness. While my grandmother Eugénie explored the bay's flora, my grandfather Félix promised himself that he would walk a lot, and so improve his health just by breathing. To be cured by breathing: a dream prescription. And their first stay there was indeed like a dream.

They rented a house a stone's throw from the Place des Palmiers (now Place Fleming), on the edge of the forest and at the foot of an enormous dune. The kind of place vulnerable to infiltration by sand and stifling in high summer. They were enchanted by it all: the house itself, low, towered over by pines and surrounded by hydrangeas; exploring the architectural marvels that so many of the Winter Town villas were; the odour of iodine and kelp, resin and pine needles; bicycle rides to the Moulleau and Abatilles beaches, my grandmother frequently falling off – even though she wasn't born in the 18th century, she still had no affinity whatsoever for any kind of sporting activity. Scared stiff, she would suddenly stop pedalling, as if to better consider this ridiculous object that she found herself straddling; but once she got going she would be so thrilled that she'd let go of the handlebars to grab a flower or wave her hand around to emphasize what she was saying. As for bathing, since neither of them could swim they delighted instead in watching their daughter as she metamorphosed into seaweed in front of their eyes. In truth, the botanical image of passively floating seaweed did not really suit the personality of their only child, who, energized by the sea air, swam, skipped and ran until she was exhausted, and, always seeking to surpass her own achievements, begged her father for a chronometer. That first summer in Arcachon, was an undreamt-of holiday for my grandparents, but for their daughter it was more like a springboard to excellence – towards a victory that one day would distinguish her. In what field? Sport, certainly. Which one? Swimming, without a shadow of a doubt. Her parents, anxious not to see her overtiring herself, tried to set boundaries. You know, her father said to her, one day you're going to have to measure your ability in group competition. She got out of the water and shook herself off.

"Groups? I don't think so." (She threw a hostile glance in the direction of the first swimming clubs that were making their way down to the beach.) "I can't bear groups," she added, quite indignant. Jackie was pretty and gifted, but entirely set against the idea of anything organized, and utterly recalcitrant when it came to being part of a team, indeed being part of anything.

She got back into the water to try and beat that day's record.

My grandparents had only one desire: to return. Which from then on they did every summer. On each visit, the garden, a slim border zone between the house and the dune, had shrunk a little more. The sand was taking over. Pine cones and needles accumulated on the roof. The hydrangeas looked sick. Inside, a layer of dusty sand covered the furniture and the floor. It squeaked beneath the soles of their shoes. Armed with dustpans and brooms, Félix and Eugénie took up the fight, disregarding the laws of physics and the inevitability of certain outcomes. The huge body of sand that towered above their heads – the same dune that would soon become a ski slope for a few daring people – seemed friendly enough to them. Endlessly sweeping sand was an undemanding occupation. It was part of their new taste for holidays, along with the banging of the shutters, opening out onto free time.

I never saw their first Arcachon house. Its precarious position was presumably what led to its destruction. But it occupied such an important place in my grandparents' stories that I came to believe it was the link to a secret, the secret of how they fell in love at first sight with the spirit of a place, and it held the clue to a mystery: the mystery of Joy. So much so that whenever I found myself at the Place des Palmiers – when I was sent to pick up some medicine from the pharmacy with the same name, or when I went over to play with a friend – I would go and look at the place where it had once stood.

When they reached retirement age they moved away from both Viroflay and the house at the foot of the dune. They moved to Arcachon full-time, first to the Villa Osseloise, on Rue de la Mairie, then to Avenue Régnault. At last they were able to enjoy all the seasons, with all their nuances and subtle shifts. They were also able to experience – something that was to fascinate me some years later – the ebb and flow of the summer crowds and the empty beaches, of sound and silence, the autumn equinox and the blossoming of the mimosa in February.

THE LIFE-SAVING WOUND

It would be an exaggeration to call the paid holiday legislation of 1936 and the effect it had on my grandparents' lives revolutionary. Firstly, in terms of the importance of holidays in their way of life, Félix and Eugénie were too happy in their day-to-day lives, too fulfilled by their routines, the byways of their love, to hail the gift of two weeks of holidays as an unprecedented liberation. Being in love is an occupation in itself, and a holiday is merely a way of expanding it. But what more than anything else prevented this law from setting off in them the thunderbolt of revolution was that Félix, a survivor of the First World War (in which some 10 million soldiers were killed), had already experienced the sudden shock of a world turned upside down. And there was nothing comparable between the discovery of leisure time and the descent into the hell of war. The fracture was already in place, brought about by horror.

He survived the bloodbath. Bombings, pursuit, bayonet in hand, hand-to-hand combat, physical contact with the enemy, their faces up against his own, their shared youth. Félix Marie Joseph, as a Christian, was sickened by having to kill. But as a patriot he believed in his mission. As he ran – choked by gas, dodging explosions and bodies as they fell to the ground – he glimpsed, high above, the glittering figure of a victorious France. She gestured to him, addressed him directly, appealed to his courage, his bravery in battle. He had no need for the numb of alcohol to help him lead his men as they scrambled over the charnel terrain. In his imagination France sometimes wore the smile of the Virgin, and when he tore his skin on barbed wire and ran like a madman, blind to the carnage, it wasn't only he who was running, but also, alongside him, invisible, inexhaustible, his childhood self, the little boy he once was, perched on his lucky star, comforted and always protected by the roadside shrines scattered all over his native Brittany. Nonetheless, he suffered a shrapnel wound in his right hip in the early days of the war, on 5th October 1914, at Beuvraignes. Was it a moment when the little boy with his lucky star, asleep on his straw mattress and blissfully deaf to the rumble of the cannons, forgot to stay by his side? On the contrary: it was this wound that saved his life. Félix was transported by stretcher to the heart of the fighting, which raged north of Beuvraignes, in the Bois des Loges: 1,857 dead, on a stretch of land 6,050 metres square. A massacre on both the German and French sides. The soldiers fought for a week without respite. Corpses piled high on the ground, covered only by clods of earth kicked up by explosions. Eugénie had no news. She knew only that the German military operation, called "the race to the sea", was appallingly deadly. She hoped for a letter, a word; she was eaten up with anguish, and finally could bear it no longer. She set off to search for her fiancé in the makeshift hospitals that were multiplying in formerly grand hotels, castles and convents. She had never left Normandy before; now she found herself frenziedly searching all over the devastated plains of the Somme. She took buses, was given lifts by peasants, got caught up in the chaos of groups of villagers fleeing the enemy, wandered through the ruins not knowing where she was heading or how she was going to get back to her parents, until one day at the end of November, in a school-turned-hospital, an amputee soldier told her that he knew Félix Charles – they were both in the 94th infantry regiment, but he had no idea what had happened to him since the nightmare battle of the Bois des Loges. That this man had seen Félix alive gave Eugénie renewed hope, and after she managed to find her way back to her father's farm she was again optimistic about the future. The first letter she received from Félix, from Montdidier, filled her with ecstatic joy. Though he was badly injured, he was going to survive. His wound was infected but he had not lost mobility in his hip. Having escaped the carnage with his life, he now understood the value of every moment wrested from death. Just like

Madame du Barry, Louis XV's favourite, condemned to the guillotine, who begged the executioner to grant her one more minute, he too prayed, begged that he be afforded a little more time, however brief; that he survive the night, that he be allowed to see the first light of the following morning. It took him many months to recover. He was officially decommissioned on 12th August 1915, with a Croix de Guerre medal and a citation: "Excellent conduct under fire. He has, with his energy and sangfroid, brilliantly defeated, with his men, an enemy attack on his division."

The very same month, October 1914, maybe even the same day that Félix Charles was struck by shrapnel and fell in woodland strewn with corpses, the writer and diplomat Paul Claudel was in Bordeaux, where he was employed in the prison service. He went for a stroll by the sea, along a beach strewn with jellyfish. "Arcachon and the Ocean again," he noted in his diary. "There are huge chunks of translucent flesh on the beach, with deep valves I can slip my fingers into." His brother-in-law, Antoine-Jean Sainte-Marie Perrin, was at the front, near Ypres, where he would be killed a few weeks later. In a letter to his parents he wrote that if he died they must not mourn, because he "will be with God, enjoying the joy that is reserved for martyrs". Claudel was of the same mind, and he experienced an immense rush of exultation. The family was informed that the young man had been wounded. In fact it wasn't true. Claudel's reaction: "The news we received about S.-M.'s health was a mistake. The gentlemen had the name wrong. It is better this way. My father-in-law's family has shown that they are deserving of this martyr." Whatever. He was alive. He wandered through the streets of Arcachon, took a boat from the jetty to Cap Ferret, followed a sandy path and ended up on a beach overlooking the Atlantic Ocean. He walked in the wind and the sun. Struck by the way the gelatinous flesh of the jellyfish reflected the light, he plunged his fingers into their holes. It was as if he were satisfying some obscene appetite, or, more symbolically, blocking – for a time and for himself – the terrifying power of the Gorgon.

Lying in agony on his hospital bed, Félix had no interest in discovering the joy reserved for martyrs. He wanted only one thing: to be healed, so that one day he would be able to walk once more in the wind and the sun.

Several buildings in Arcachon served as makeshift hospitals and sanatoriums during the 1914–18 war. It never occurred to my grandfather, when he first came to the town more than twenty years later, to try and identify them. He would whistle as he pedalled past the Grand Hotel, the Saint-Elme school, the Saint-Joseph Sanatorium, the Mauresque casino, the Saint-Dominique convent, all of which had taken in the wounded. He saw the buildings only in the present. He was alive and it was summer. The only thought he held on to from the hell he had endured was the idea that an injury could be life-saving. An acknowledgement, a sense of benediction. He limped up the steps of the Church of Our Lady and prayed to the statue of the Virgin saved from the waves by Thomas Illyricus, the Franciscan founder of the town. The statue is made of alabaster, with a pale blue veil and a faded crown that still sits squarely on her head. With one hand she cradles the baby Jesus. Her other hand is broken. Our Lady of Arcachon is barely older than an adolescent. Félix lit a candle. "Oh my Mother and my Queen, with what joy I prostrate myself at your feet! Star of the sea, guide the sailor over the abyss, and lead him to port; Saviour of Christians, keep our families safe, protect our children, bring us joy, comfort those who weep."

He loved the perfumed air, and he loved the fact that Our Lady of Arcachon was the survivor of a shipwreck. Being a survivor makes you more sensitive to the sweetness of living things.

THE BLUE OF THE LAKE

If Jackie never dreamt of looking below her as she swam, or of deciphering beneath her elegant shadow the waterline of the layers of the past, and still less of hunting down relics from the 18th century, it was because she had inherited from her father the choice of being in the present; not only did swimming, her vocation, belong in the moment, but also, as she often said, *other people's histories don't interest me.*

As for her own history, did that interest her? Of course it did, but she had no desire to turn it into a story. Even more profoundly, she saw no *history* in it. She only ever mentioned a few rare episodes, never the same ones, incidentally, as those told by her mother. This one, for example: how during one summer in Charavines, in the last months of her pregnancy, she swam every day in Lake Paladru, known as the "blue lake" – crystalline blue – and while she swam she intoned, like a nursery rhyme or an ode to the spirit of the place, *please let my child's eyes be the same colour as this lake.* She was slim and strong. She had barely put on any weight during her pregnancy.

She wore a brown cotton one-piece bathing suit that showed off her tan, with a red and purple band that drew attention to her rounded belly. She laughed a lot, and sang. She said "my child" without being able to specify "my son" or "my daughter". Her doctor didn't do ultrasounds; back then if people wanted to try and predict a baby's sex it could only be done through superstition and old wives' tales. Jackie didn't want to predict anything. She lived in the bubble of her present, as I lived in the bubble of her body. The lake was cooler than the clear liquid I swam in – better that way round than the other, since however fanatical my mother was about swimming she didn't stay in the lake day and night, while for me the amniotic cavity was my only home.

It was hot that summer in Charavines. Since 8th May France had been celebrating the Liberation, or, more precisely, tending its wounds. My mother never was able to tell me anything about what was going on elsewhere in France, in Europe, in the world. She was as inarticulate on such matters and as removed from current events as the fish in the lake. She stayed with the tench, the carp and the trout in their instinctive forward movement, their sensation of depth and lightness, their blindness, the graze of a frond of seaweed, the bobbing of a small boat, the tempest of an oar stroking the water. She swam with the fish and I swam with her. Day after day she abandoned herself to the lake water and I to the amniotic fluid. I inhabited her rhythm. We floated, together.

There is nothing more to this episode: she was pregnant with me, she swam, she dreamt of the colour my eyes would be. Barely even an episode, more of an evocation. And, unlike during her holidays in Arcachon, where it is easy for me to imagine her as she got out of the water and ran towards the towel that her mother held out for her, there, during the summer that she awaited my arrival, I have never been able to picture anyone else on the bank.

THE SUITCASE-CRADLE

Gravida, heavy, weighed down with a gestating baby; she was not that. The lake supported my weight. She progressed, buoyant, in her pregnancy. She swam right up to the limit of what was possible, only returning to join her husband at the beginning of autumn, driven away by the mists and the water that had grown too cold to swim in. Perhaps she resisted the temptation to let their love affair dissipate in the blue of the lake. A temptation, nothing more, for I was born in Lyon in October.

I was born under the spell of the music and gentle sway of the mingled waters of my mother and the lake, the first barely tinged by the faintest hint of acidity, the second totally neutral. I emerged in a city through which two rivers run. I was born, like my mother, in the aftermath of a war. In a city where all the bridges had been destroyed by the Germans in their flight from the advancing French troops, a city where there was a violent ongoing settling of scores between collaborators and those who had been in the Resistance (Jackie was aware of, but not particularly bothered by, the sound of people running over the rooftops and gunshots), a city above all where Armand, my father, could not get the fighting out of his head. He was unable to let go of the fear, of the nights when, carrying messages concealed in his bicycle, he would hurtle down hills, listening out for every sound as he cycled along the mountain roads and through the woods, bypassing ghostly villages at the first inkling of dawn. He could not let go of the memory, the obsessive fear he felt in Lyon under German occupation, the torture and executions, but he also remembered the explosion of joy when he realized, after several nights of fighting, uncertain advances, misfired gunshots, being pursued through the warren of streets with their closed shutters and rolled-down awnings, then darting down into underground passageways, that they had won.

As soon as I was born Jackie checked the colour of my eyes. I cannot believe that in the first minutes of my life they really were the same blue as that of the lake in which she swam all summer, but they seemed so to her when the baby was placed in her arms. She loved to talk about that holiday in Charavines, and then, without any transition, the moment when she realized that her wish had been granted, the story was over. For example, the reason she and my father decided to leave Lyon was never discussed. They left in spite of the fact that just before I was born she had applied for a secretarial job. It was obvious that even had the response been positive, she had already ruled out the secretarial job in favour of the lake. Stranger still, they decided to leave Lyon even though my father had found work there and was attached to the city, bound by the dangers he had lived through during the war – and perhaps by something else, or someone else. But that could never be talked about, even less than questions about work, either by him or by her. Jackie once said that when she first set foot in their tiny apartment in Lyon, 120 Rue de Sully, it was clear that no one actually lived there; the only piece of furniture, leaning against the wall, was Armand's bicycle.

"And what did you think?"

"Nothing. Maybe that I'd married someone who didn't like being inside. It didn't bother me. Comfort never mattered very much to me."

But when there is a child you do need to arrange a home a little. Jackie couldn't do it, and so she asked her mother for help. Faced with the blatant ineptitude of a couple who wanted to spend all their time out of doors, my grandmother took action. In the middle of winter she turned up in Lyon to collect me. She had prepared a small suitcase, snugly lined with woollens, to be my cradle during the long journey to Arcachon.

Instead of feeling relieved, the new parents seemed to become even more restless. With a kind of fanaticism they took up their sporting activities from the time of their engagement. Cycling, skiing, tennis. They smashed the ball back and forth to each other. They played tennis in a city and a world in ruins. Armand took it frighteningly seriously; during these matches, played in the period immediately after his experience running missions as a messenger in the Resistance, he was feeling his way around another silence, not the silence of underground fighting and solitary fear, but the silence between a couple, which presented itself in quite contradictory ways. My father kept his thoughts to himself. My mother was irrepressibly cheerful. It is possible that with the first days of spring, the blooming of the wild lilacs and the joy of simply watching the green flowing waters of the River Saône, they were feeling so secure and joyful in their bodies that they exchanged heartfelt *I love you*s on the bridges that were being rebuilt. They must have walked a lot and fallen asleep at night in a tense exhaustion easily confused with desire. I was born out of athletic instincts and the lustful desire between perfect bodies. I was born to parents who met at the age of fifteen and who had not matured at the same rate during their enforced wartime separation. It was as if only my father had grown older. One evening in January 1945 he stood waiting for Jackie among snow-covered rubble on the platform of the Perrache train station, beneath the cracked arch and the large clock that had been knocked off-kilter; he had no memory of the teenager he had once been, while the bubbly young woman in red boots with wooden soles and woollen socks who threw her arms around his neck had barely changed at all.

My grandmother wrote them detailed letters about my daily life, to which my grandfather sometimes added a snatch of poetry: a seagull walking by the water's edge, a flight of doves, a sandbank appearing like a ghost. My mother learnt these lines of poetry by heart. She erased the mystical dimension, translating it into an urge to move, to run along the sand and stretch out in the sun. Jackie and Armand read the letters without comment. They avoided the question: stay in Lyon, or move to Arcachon? My father thought he would die of boredom living year round in a seaside resort and that the suitcase that had been used for my departure could serve just as well for my return, but my mother wanted only two things: to be near her parents, and to spend her life on holiday in Arcachon.

My grandmother never tired of telling the story of the suitcase. Laughing, she would show me the suitcase, which later became the receptacle that held her knitting and balls of wool. A suitcase made of brown cardboard, lined with paper printed with a lighter brown pattern that I continued to believe – because Eugénie was an excellent storyteller? Because I really remembered it so? – was an expensive, elaborately flocked fabric wall covering. A "post-war" suitcase I would call it, as Charles-Albert Cingria named his bed "late Marie-Antoinette", and then "the Terror". My suitcase-cradle was typical of the era's shabbiness and austerity, though there was nothing that said "terror" about it. It was "love". I used to imagine that my passion for travel had its origins in the long train journey from Lyon to Arcachon, in the total trust in which I was cradled, in the softness of the touch of the stack of woollens, the deliciousness of sleeping while moving, and, when gentle hands lifted me from my suitcase-cradle and sat me down in front of the window, in the thrilling sight of a world that was as alluring as it was untouchable. While my grandmother, in her guileless way, spun me the saga of an act that resembled a kidnapping, I would tell myself that that was how I discovered the art of departure. I decided that I would be both the traveller and her baggage, and every time I left I would take myself with me. Of course, in reality it was only many years later that I was able to tell myself that. When I began to imagine what lay beyond the bay. When I began to be piqued by the urge to explore other coastlines, to compare grains of sand from different beaches and the colours of the setting sun, waves rolling one after another, leaping like the wild horses of the Apocalypse or smooth and flawless as a mirror... That was when the suitcase-cradle began to take shape as a symbol of my future. But at the very beginning, in the first months when I was discovering life, and when, as soon as the air was warm enough, they began to take me to the beach, it would be more accurate to see in the suitcase-cradle something of Noah's Ark. A minuscule hull, magically unsinkable. The woollens from the train journey replaced by cork panels.

The gorse and broom with their yellow flowers. I was set down at the water's edge. Overnight the suitcase-cradle became my boat.

THE YOUNG MAN STOPPED IN HIS TRACKS

Jackie didn't wait long before leaving to join her parents, suitcase and child. She left Lyon without looking back, confident that her husband would follow her. In Arcachon they planned to buy a tandem and take up their sporting activities again. If being in love is not so much looking at one another but rather facing the same way together, then the tandem is the ideal vehicle for love. One behind the other, pedalling in concert in the same direction, they were going to gobble up the kilometres. (Fortunately the region is flat.) They sent each other love letters. She was tanned all over when she went to meet him at the little train station in Arcachon. He smiled but was more taciturn than ever. In reality he never completely left Lyon. He kept a little distance from her, a withdrawal. Slipped between the pages of his favourite book, *Premier de cordée,* by the great French mountaineer Frison-Roche, was a piece of paper folded in two, signed by the president of the Liberation Committee of the 3rd arrondissement in Lyon and dated 7th February 1945, certifying that "Monsieur Thomas

Armand took part in the Liberation of Lyon as a messenger for the Resistance." The piece of paper had none of the brilliance of a formal recognition; for him it was just a bookmark. He took no pride in this war, the Second World War. It had the bitter aftertaste of a defeat poorly disguised as victory. Unlike Félix's, his body bore no trace. He was physically unscathed, but his personality, already inclined to taciturnity, now definitively took on this characteristic. Closed in and protected by his silence, he was both present and absent: a combination to which only he possessed the key. At least he believed he did; but the walls of silence imprison us no less than they protect us.

Last stop, Arcachon. Everybody off! "The train goes no farther, after that it's sand and ocean," said my mother cheerfully. It was the end of the line. He embraced his young wife, touched her bare shoulder, planted a kiss on her rosy lips. They left the station and walked away, unaware that they were walking over the underground cells of the Germans' headquarters, abandoned in haste, everything left just as it was.

A few years ago, sitting at a pavement café opposite the Théâtre des Célestins in Lyon on a particularly clear spring evening, I saw the silhouette of a young man standing in front of the theatre. And with that strange effect of anticipation that makes us immediately complicit with phantom apparitions and open to hearing the message that their return signals they have come to deliver, I knew straightaway it was my father, my father when he was a young man. A thick, wavy lock of light brown hair fell across his forehead. He wore golfing trousers and a dark blue shirt, and clunky shoes that made him look so obviously from the 1940s. They were brown, like my suitcase-cradle. To my spellbound eyes it was clear that the shoes and suitcase must have coexisted in the small apartment at 120 Rue de Sully. There can be complicity between objects, too. These two, shoes and suitcase, used to keep company and must have witnessed scenes that will always be hidden from me. He had been running. He was trying to catch his breath. He didn't say anything to me. He didn't want to talk. But, just as he always had during his short life, he managed to make me feel I existed for him in a way that no one else did, and to communicate precisely, even without words, what he was feeling. He stood there, his back to the facade of the Théâtre des Célestins, fully present and alive, unmoving. His blue eyes seemed to be watching out for a pursuer. They scanned the adjacent narrow streets. Or perhaps, because streets are also mirrors, his eyes reflected back to him this truth: the young man stopped in his tracks is you. The war is over. No one seeks your death any more. It will only come from you. And it's not an insignificant danger. Stop looking behind you. No one is after you any more. Look inside you. See the trap you've set yourself.

I could hear his thoughts as clearly as if I were inside his head. I watched him closely. He didn't have that air of sadness that I had always known in him, or those three fine lines at the corner of each eye. I held my breath. I was stunned, yet at the same time it seemed to me that there was nothing surprising about the situation, even if finding myself suddenly sharing his space and his youth made my heart beat faster, and confirmed an intuition that had come to me very early on: the certainty that the day I was born his future had slammed shut. Is that a little bit true of every birth? I don't know, but for my father – aged twenty, only recently seized by that fever for discovery that was part and parcel of his astonishment at still being alive, at having survived the carnage of the Second World War – the birth of a child killed any impetus for the future. His love might have been no more than a teenage fling. If there hadn't been a child he would have been free to see where this love might lead; and if it didn't go very far, he might have had the courage to end it. Jackie, with her beauty and her love of singing, would have got over it; she might even have been obscurely relieved. But with a newborn baby, a little girl who had his eyes, this child whom he recognized and in whom he recognized himself, the die was cast.

By an irony of history, the Institute of Human Sciences in Lyon where I work is on the very site where the Gestapo was once headquartered under the command of Klaus Barbie. Every time I go down to the basement to sit in a small room with my colleagues and consider and discuss Voltaire's satirical writings, or the inflammatory rhetoric of the Revolutionary pamphlet *Old Man Duchesne*, I have visions of bodies being tortured, Jews, members of the Resistance, men and women being beaten with fists or batons. They are revived with buckets of water and it starts again: their nails are pulled out, they're burned with blowtorches, tortured by drowning, the soles of their feet are slashed with razorblades and they are forced to walk on salt. Their screams drown out the lecturer's voice, traces of blood that have not been completely absorbed by the stones on the ground seep up the walls, and then the screams stop, the blood vanishes and I manage somehow to recapture the thread of the lecture.

A CHAMPION IN THE MAKING

Jackie returned to Arcachon in holiday mode. She and her husband moved into the ground floor of her parents' new house, which, unlike their first house on the edge of the forest, was in Summer Town, just outside Winter Town. She heard, or imagined, their footsteps above her head, and through the open windows the mingled voices of her father and mother, background noise as vital to her as the air that she breathed. If she went out into the garden she could join in their conversation just by casting a few words upwards through the foliage. My bedroom was upstairs on the first floor. I let out a stream of delighted babbling, proof of my attraction to the spoken life of my family and the concert of birds chirping in the sky.

By the time she woke up my father had already left for work (as a graphic artist for the shipbuilding company Couach, then, a few months later, in the nearby town of Facture, in the offices of the paper factory Pine Cellulose; jobs in this town of spas and retirees, when they weren't something to do with tourism, had something clandestine about them). She got dressed and went down to the sea. Her father came with her. They had adopted the rhythm of the trainer with his future champion. The quest for a split second. He was strict: that was what she wanted. There was something fanatical in her craving for excellence. He timed her, critiqued her style with a focus on improving it. She listened; her dedication to swimming was absolute. In the evening over dinner all they talked about was that day's performance. My father's taciturnity intensified. In the midst of family life, without actually challenging it, he was retrenching himself in silence as though inside a completely separate life. Without anything being said, the idea of the tandem was abandoned. It was literally dead in the water. Meanwhile my mother worried: now it was the summer, but how long would she be able to make the summer last, if there was no departure date to bring it to an end? It depends, she was told. It depended on her as well. There were some years when the water was perfect right up until the end of October or even later. This heartened her a little, but then after that, how much time would she have to kill before she could begin training again? The responses she got were encouraging: here the spring is never far away, and with the arrival of spring the water rapidly warms up. It's a mild climate. Nothing changes in the pine forests. Winter barely makes a mark.

Still, night was beginning to fall earlier and earlier, and one day, as she was pushing the pram along the

Boulevard de la Plage, she shivered in the damp breeze. It wasn't cold: autumn announces itself gradually. She was shivering for no reason. If you were to ask her to explain why, she would have said it was the *uncertainty*.

Had she inquired about the dates and location of the championship? She would have had no answer to such a question. She'd have let go of the pram in astonishment. She had come back to Arcachon so that she could continue being on holiday. She had placed all her faith in Summer Town. Competition, unless it was against herself and for her sole witness, her father – trainer, judge and spectator all at once – repulsed her to her very core. It was unbearable to her. My grandmother told me that when she was a child, although Jackie was so much quicker than all the other children when it came to understanding and memorizing, as soon as she was asked to write an essay or sit a test she'd be overcome with irrational anxiety. She would cry and shake, sob that she was going to die. These hysterics stirred up ill feeling among the other children. Raising the spectre of death in the midst of a group of schoolchildren struggling with their multiplication tables or trying to make the past participle agree devalued the test. The problems they were working away at became ridiculous.

Jackie was allergic to all forms of ranking. That didn't stop her worshipping the Olympic swimmer, dreaming of becoming a champion. "I would trade all the poetry of Baudelaire for a female Olympic swimmer," wrote Céline. She would certainly have applauded this statement. She didn't need to have read *Les Fleurs du mal* to be entirely in agreement.

CRAWLING

In long-standing tradition, at the beginning of July, a row of tents was pitched on Arcachon beach. They were made of striped canvas and pitched along a line parallel to the sea. An area the size of a small awning separated each one from the next. People use them primarily for getting changed, but also for napping, reading or playing cards in the shade. I was fascinated by the tents' interiors. As soon as my mother or grandmother lost sight of me I would set off to explore, crawling from one tent to the next. Thanks to my size and stealth I was able to slip unnoticed into the alluringly hospitable amber shadows. I made my way at ankle height, never reaching above calf height. I stole past men contorting themselves as they pulled on their trunks, women undoing their bras and fervently rubbing on sun cream. I slipped between legs, brushed against body hair, inhaled the odour of moist nudity, breathing in the droplets.

One of the attractions of these perambulations was their distinctive atmosphere. But the sand inside was the same as the sand outside. So, careful to remain unnoticed by these giants with their careless movements, I continued on my way, pushing against the sand and then relaxing into it, ploughing my knees and forearms into its powdery softness, always with my eye on the next tent and the grotesque movements going on inside. Crawling has plenty of things going for it. To the point that I even wondered whether learning to walk would really be worth the effort.

I didn't limit myself to crawling among the orange-and-white striped tents. I explored out in the open too. I scuttled towards the water with the same energy and, since there was no one to stop me, less cunning. And now that I was no longer going from tent to tent, I allowed myself the luxury of pausing wherever I wanted, going up to parents and children to play with their buckets and spades, trampling all over their towels. That was the most delicious thing. I loved the sand, but I adored these multi-coloured islands of spongy fabric. I'd lie down and then get up and drag the towel off with me. Until my mother or grandmother stopped me, or sometimes the owner of the towel. A little embarrassed to be arguing in public with a toddler over a towel, but there you go. The kind of situation that grown-ups, with their huge feet, hands like paddles, and whale-like bellies, are so masterful at dropping themselves in. The unbelievable size of their feet: I don't quite know why, but it was when they were half buried in the sand and then all of a sudden they uncovered them that I noticed how enormous they really were. I saw it later too, when we got home and the big people, the really big people, sat down on a bench to wipe the sand from between their toes. There ought to be a special brush for de-sanding the extremities. That would be really useful. They were extremely fussy about it. Is it allowed to bring sand into the house? No, it is absolutely forbidden. What about seaweed, is that allowed? No, but it doesn't matter as much. So I kept the narrow fragments of black ribbon that stuck to my skin like a tattoo of the day.

My route to the sea never covered the same distance. It would be long or short depending on the tide. At low tide I would head towards the sea but it was never certain that I would reach it. It was so far that there were an infinite number of possible detours and distractions.

If I resisted the pleasure of plunging my face into the kelp or paddling in the warm waters of a tide pool, if I avoided the lure of an unfamiliar towel, sometimes there was the opportunity for a different kind of adventure, a boat marooned on the sand. Tilted at an angle, it was ideal for climbing, and if I crouched down inside, underneath one of the wooden benches, they'd never find me.

On the way down to the water anything was possible, even the most surprising thing of all, this moment of spontaneity: meeting another child, finding my presence absorbed by the gaze of another.

While I was crawling along the beach, captivated by the next episode of the infinitely changing wonders scattered across the sand, my mother had disappeared. She had gone for a swim. She was swimming the crawl; she was crawling too, but in the water. I remained perfectly calm at the sight of my mother walking towards the water to bathe. I didn't belong to that category of children who howl as soon as their mother makes a move to leave them. I identified with her pleasure. Obviously we weren't crawling in the same element, but, for her as for me, it was a vital occupation. Though our harmony was less symbiotic than it was when I was a foetus growing inside her, protected by the double confinement of her body and the lake, it was still beyond doubt.

THE CHILDREN FROM ELSEWHERE

We, the children of the shore, had a sense of superiority to the children from elsewhere. They always arrived at the same time, either 1st July or 1st August. They left together at the same time too. It was unheard of for a vacationing child to be so desperate to stay that the parents, either obligingly or simply because they hadn't the strength to resist caving in to the force of the child's determination, decided to delay the date of their return. Or even decided never to return to the shuttered house they had left behind. How was it possible, I wondered, to live for a month in this beautiful place and then leave as planned, as if nothing had happened? They were astonished at my astonishment. "We're on holiday," they would say. They seemed to think this was an explanation.

The children from elsewhere were very pale. Their mothers were endlessly running after them to put more sun cream on their shoulders and their sun hats back on their heads. I wondered why they bothered, for it was never any use. The little holidaymakers always ended up peeling. And on top of that, everything terrified them, everything disgusted them. They stared, repulsed, at the enormous jellyfish washed up on the sand, those great masses of passive transparency with absolutely no instinct to harm (though none of the children ever thought of poking their fingers inside them like Paul Claudel did!). They shrieked when they saw the little green crabs amiably busying themselves as they shuffled slantwise along the shore. Some of them were not equipped for summer when they arrived; they would turn up off the train, little boys in closed shoes and long trousers, little girls in dresses with bows in their hair.

The children from elsewhere looked anxiously around at this new world. They needed time to understand. Understand what? Why, everything! Why does the sea pull back so far and then return? What does the moon have to do with it? Why is the passage from sand to water uninterrupted, not broken by a step like the edge of a swimming pool? Where do waves come from? Why do some bodies float and not others (theirs, for example)? Why don't fish make any sound?

And why is the water salty? A little African boy called Alain had the answer: he was convinced that the sea is full of monsters and if it's salty, it's from their victims' tears. I was about to try and put him right and then I stopped: his terror was written all over his face.

We, the children of the shore, ran everywhere, turning like dervishes from one activity to another. Equipped with nets, we fished for crabs, starfish and seahorses. Tiny shrimp slipped through the mesh, but we didn't care. To catch a razor clam you have to spot the hole in the sand that shows you where it is, then pour in salt and wait for the silly razor clam to emerge. There were cockles, mussels and other clams too.

The children from elsewhere knew none of this.

Our sense of superiority applied even in response to tragic local events. When we heard about another accidental drowning, we thought: How could they have been so stupid! Our scorn was never more crushing than for the children from elsewhere at summer camp. They stood in line and sang; we almost pitied them. It was a given that we would never play with them. This wasn't true for the other vacationing children. In reality most of them tanned and loosened up pretty quickly. They picked things up at a faster rate than the summer went by. And often their wild questions gave us ideas. In the gangs that came together and fell apart, everyone soon forgot who came from where and how long they were staying. No one bothered with formalities like name and age when it came to playing together. We built sandcastles with crenellations and turrets, moats and drawbridges. When the moats were dry they were ineffectual, but the rising tide turned them into formidable defences. The castle became impregnable. But it never lasted long. The very tide that protected it from the enemy soon became its worst enemy. It engulfed the foundations (the dungeons where traitors were left to rot!), and quickly reached the ramparts. With tiny, lapping waves the sea razed the moats, ate into the turrets and crenellations. The cracks widened. Great chunks sheered off. The splendid castle was subsiding into a heap of sand. Battered, a whole side collapsed. The heavy-hearted builders couldn't bear to accept it. Focused and full of hope, I ran around stopping up the cracks with sea foam, while the boys rushed around rebuilding the roof, smoothing it down with a spade. "We must build a dam to save the castle!" one of them said. I didn't think it would work. It was too late. I gave up on the sea foam, abandoned the builders and joined in the modest activity of a pair of twins making patty cakes out of damp sand. The two little girls were completely identical, just like their patty cakes.

The castle continued to crumble.

"You should have built it on the dry sand there, where the tide doesn't reach," pontificated one of the fathers, overlooking our attraction to lost causes and the empire of ruins. It was precisely because the sandcastle was collapsing – this was in the brief interval when, in its very dilapidation, it revealed the traces of its former glory – that suddenly it came alive and was *inhabited*. It echoed with voices, cries for help, history – and *we* were struck by a great wave of sadness. I left the twin pastry chefs and their cake tins and went back to join the band of defeated builders.

Children from elsewhere, children who counted off their days at the beach, for whom a wasted morning was irretrievable: in truth, I was no different from you. Even if I got there before you and was still going to be there after you left, I was no more relaxed about it than you. Anything that made me late leaving for the beach filled me with rage, a secret, silent rage. When it came to the division of roles, tantrums, raised voices, outpourings of noisy emotion, it was my mother's voice that was heard. Jackie was not as reserved as I; if she wasn't able to swim because of some obligation or because of what she called "bad weather" (wind or waves), she cried. She had no qualms when it came to overtly expressing her unhappiness. It always took me a little by surprise, but I didn't reproach her for it. On the contrary, I would have loved to be able to dare to express the pain that was eating at me. I admired her for having absolutely no interest in aping other grown-ups. Once, when I went over to her with an armful of dolls and asked her to play with me, she answered, kindly: "You know, I don't like playing with other children."

I envied her, I admired her, and I approved of her. The beach brought us together. I was in my own world, as she said. And she was in hers. Her parents watched us from a distance. Apart from when she was caught up in her obsession with beating her own record, and her father, a strict coach, carefully marked out the curve of her average speeds.

My mother was a child apart.

A summertime child, definitively uncoupled from any notion of return.

INVISIBLE FRONTIERS

As well as ensuring the colour of my eyes by immersing herself in the blue waters of the lake in Charavines, my mother had another favourite anecdote, not about a magical transfiguration this time, but a panic. It took place when she was young, in her very first home, the house in Versailles on Rue Sainte-Adélaïde. She was whining to her parents, whimpering about how unhappy she was, that she was going to die. Rolling around on the floor, she grabbed a corner of the tablecloth and smashed a vase. She filled the room with her wailing. Her mother was used to it. Her father had had more than enough. He took her by the arm, opened the front door and pushed her out into the street. "If you're not happy here with us, go." She had been abandoned! The horror! She was seized by a dread that crushed her heart like an enormous claw.

"An iron claw, like an instrument of torture. I thought it was all over: I was on the street, thrown out by my parents."

"So what did you do?"

"I carried on weeping and howling. After a little while – it felt like a century – my father opened the door."

"There must be plenty of empty bedrooms in the Palace of Versailles, you could easily have found a way to sneak in. Maybe there was even an orphanage nearby. They'd have taken you in."

She looked at me oddly.

"Because you walk around with the address of an orphanage in your pocket... Do you really think I was that kind of child?"

I wondered what she meant by "that kind of child". I knew that she was aware of one of my peculiar habits: I never went into a room without first checking that there was a window in case I needed to escape. That meant some bathrooms and toilets were out of bounds to me. On the other hand, I could always escape from anywhere I found myself.

"I had nowhere to go. The only place I knew was my parents' house. That terror when I found myself outside the front door, slammed shut, just thinking about it..."

The only house she knew was her parents' house. Years later she was gripped by the same fear when, after living so long under their wing, it came to setting up her own home. It was if her father had taken her by the arm and thrown her out again, cast her once more from the nest. It was cold and dark. She wept, lost in a tenebrous garden. The only light in the whole world shone out from the windows of her parents' house.

Her house, 14 Rue Nathaniel-Johnston, in Autumn Town, where she might have quite enjoyed playing at being a young housewife, was not, in reality, very far from her parents' house on Avenue Régnault. *In reality*. In her head it was quite different. She felt abandoned. What use was a house if her mother and father didn't live there? I was sad too not to be living with my grandfather, in the enclave of his imagination, in the unpredictable, searing zone where I never knew if he was making things up or telling the truth ("Who told you it's more truthful when nothing's invented? Who told you it's even possible to talk without making things up?" Félix would say with a smile, exacerbating my confusion). I missed Félix, but the attraction of the new is powerful too, and then, even when he wasn't there, his stories were always with me.

I was concerned that our new address was in Autumn Town. Arcachon is famously divided into Winter Town, Summer Town, Autumn Town and Spring Town. I understood this division into four neighbourhoods or seasons literally. Félix used to tell me this story: how the transition from one to another, from Winter Town to Summer Town, from Summer Town to Autumn Town or Spring Town, happens without you noticing. Now that I know the area, I told myself, I understand. It would never have occurred to me – I would never have been so stupid – to go wandering among the piles of dead leaves in Autumn Town after a gorgeous day at the beach, or to ferret about in Winter Town. But every summer there are always a few tourists who fall into the trap. They find themselves, clad in nothing but their swimsuits, wandering around in the freezing fog. Shivering, they try to find their way through the icy mist that has long fallen on Winter Town. They walk past Café Repetto without stopping, past the Bistro des Marins, the Church of Our Lady, the Place des Palmiers. They stop at the Café of the Clairvoyants of the Future, where they pay no attention to the shrewd predictions of the well-oiled regulars (wise men, my grandfather taught me, are not always easy to spot at first glance). They take a break, of course, at the Bar of the Forgotten, where the tanked-up graduates of the School of the Sloshed hang out, though that's unlikely to be much use either... Completely oblivious, off they go merrily into the forest. And then, just a few steps in, a bitter chill freezes them to the bone. Poor things – they have almost no chance of finding their way back. After they've been missing for two or three days their landlady sticks up a "for rent" sign over the window of the room where they barely slept... I would listen to him, half-believing, half-disbelieving. We had a game where we would stare at people walking past and try to guess which of them would never take such a stupid risk, and which ones looked like they might cross the invisible line.

Getting lost in the freezing forest was a grim prospect, and I was the first to take it seriously. But there was another eventuality, which was even worse. Occasionally a group of unfortunate tourists, arms laden with parasols, folding chairs and towels, would venture down the "alley with no name" between the heath and the cemetery. Sometimes Félix replaced *heath* with *moorland* and *cemetery* with *bog*: "They ventured down the 'alley with no name', between moorland and bog." This version, perhaps because of the word *bog,* which sounded to me like a place where a person would literally be bogged down, dragged to the bottom of a bog, always had me on the brink of tears. Between moorland and bog, they had absolutely no chance of survival. They would simply walk, and walk, and walk. The path was desolate, and led nowhere.

"Nowhere? You're sure?"

My grandfather remained silent. He rolled himself a cigarette and stared through the tendrils of smoke into the sad destiny of these lost souls.

Sometimes I played devil's advocate. I tried to see with my own eyes, to verify with my own hand the border between the seasons. But that was the tricky part: the borders were invisible, the crossings imperceptible, as my grandfather pointed out. I'd insist: there are never such extreme differences in temperature. It's not like you ever walk straight from blue sky into a hailstorm.

And why is it you never read about these mysterious vanishing tourists in the newspaper?

"How could one talk about such things in a place which only has tourism and oysters! There are secret codes; the tourist office has its agents." I persisted, I contested, he argued back (the endless debates were part of the game).

Yet something inside me was deeply disturbed and I couldn't stop myself from thinking that even if summer and winter seem to be quite different seasons, the move from one neighbourhood to another plants deep within us the seeds of another season, dormant at first, only gradually becoming visible and growing into something fundamental to our identity. It doesn't happen to everyone. Some are more susceptible to it than others. My mother, after her defenceless youth, would later become the ideal subject. She had left summer behind – high summer, the innocent abandon of days as smooth and golden as her bronzed skin – in the house of laughter and warmth. The house in Summer Town, the house of her parents' love. On the other side of the invisible frontier.

The removal men had left. My mother was sitting on a packing crate, contemplating the empty space. A gust of damp air blew through a half-open French window in one of the bedrooms at the front of the house. I went outside to look at the garden. It was raised, on the slope of what must once have been a small hill. Behind the house a fig tree grew, its seductive scent enveloping me in a disorienting sensuality. I didn't know how to say it but I sensed that though I had crossed the border I hadn't in fact lost sight of summer. Autumn Town hadn't brought me closer to winter. It wasn't dangerous. Not only that but I owed to it my first words in a foreign language, *Nathaniel Johnston*, my first words in English. Nathaniel, a name that I had trouble pronouncing and which still sounds enigmatic to me. This touch of foreignness to my ears added to the exoticism of the move. A false foreignness, or rather a foreignness that is lodged right in the heart of Bordeaux and its vineyards, because, as I was to find out later when I went to study in Bordeaux, Nathaniel Johnston was Scottish. He was born into a family of wealthy merchants who had been living in the Gironde since the beginning of the 18th century. A politician during the reign of Napoleon III (whose friend he was), a keen horseman with his own stud farm, administrator of the Southern Railway Company, and above all passionate about viticulture (he owned, among others, Château Dauzac and Château Ducru-Beaucaillou, castles that were certainly not made of sand). It was Nathaniel Johnston who pointed the way for me, when we moved to the street that bore his name, to Bordeaux, to its history and that of Arcachon, for he was also the founder of the Ocean Fisheries, which led to my new beach, at the end of Rue George-V, alongside the fisheries building. But nobody uttered a word of any of this to me. My parents had *14 Rue Nathaniel-Johnston* printed on their visiting cards but they never asked themselves a single question about the name. Moving from Summer Town to Autumn Town was to have an impact on my mother's mental health, but it in no way altered my parents' mutual indifference to the place where they lived. They both, in their different ways, were completely uninterested in learning anything about it. They didn't read the local newspaper, didn't make friends with Arcachon families, weren't interested in finding out about their surroundings – and, of course, they didn't speak with the local accent. I refrained from asking them questions, particularly about anything to do with the town, the painstaking exploration of which, along with the techniques of storytelling, was to become a lifelong passion. *Why* wasn't in my vocabulary. Sometimes I worried about them. What if they were no smarter than those calamitous tourists, what if – even now they had made Arcachon their adopted home – they too were to find themselves condemned to wander between moorland and bog, to walk endlessly back and forth along the grey shingle "alley with no name"?

BIG DOLL

There were no grocery shops in our neighbourhood, or any other shops, and my mother had no desire to go farther afield. Shopping was a chore to her, not a diversion. It was only a short trip by bicycle for her father to bring round meals prepared by her mother or baskets of produce from the market. She could have bought sardines from a vendor who peddled his wares through the streets, crying, "Sardines, delicious sardines fresh from the bay!" but then she would have had to cook them. There was a woman who came round selling vegetables from a cart painted green. My mother remained stubbornly unmoved by its picturesque charm.

Cracks appeared in her convictions. It was beginning to seem less than certain, in spite of what she had been promised when she arrived, that living in Arcachon meant enjoying an unbroken run of gorgeous weather. I tried to keep her from losing faith in what they told her: the people were right, no one had lied to her. "Look, Mama, see the yellow butterflies in the garden, lemon yellow butterflies! Winter is over! We've only just put our swimming costumes away and it's already time to unpack our summer clothes again!"

In my bedroom, I placed my straw hat on the head of Big Doll, the forebear of all my dolls, the porcelain beauty with amber eyes. The hat completely swamped her head, like a bell, right down to her chin. Big Doll prayed as eagerly as my mother for the speedy return of the summer sun. Not for the sun, but to be rid of the hat. It kept her from seeing anything and flattened her hair, chestnut ringlets that tumbled in spirals down her ivory lace blouse. Big Doll – this has to be pointed out, since it is quite as impossible as imagining her on a pedalo – had *zero* desire to go to the beach. Just the thought of the sand insinuating itself into her articulations made her feel faint. Big Doll was a lot more coherent than half the people around me. They wanted a beach without sand, sea without salt, the ocean without waves. She completely understood that you have to want it *all*.

Big Doll was a creature of the shade. Through her, just as through the name of Nathaniel Johnston, I had a link, though I wasn't yet aware of it, with the 19th century. The presence of Big Doll in my bedroom connected me to that era. For before she was the forebear of my dolls she was the forebear of the dolls that belonged to my mother (who, when she wasn't actively abusing them, forgot them in a corner of her room, or left them somewhere in the gardens of Versailles – on the

Orangerie staircase, or on the edge of the pool called the Pièce d'eau des Suisses), of my grandmother Eugénie's dolls, and before that of the dolls that belonged to my great-grandmother Zélie. All this to say that porcelain-pale Big Doll, who had lips that parted to allow a glimpse of her sharp little teeth and eyes that closed on their own when she lay down, did not possess a bathing costume. A bathing costume! What an anachronism! Even the 26-year-old widow Marie-Caroline of Naples, Duchess of Berry, whose dip at Dieppe on 3rd August 1824 was an event of historic proportions (at the exact moment when she took her first *dip in the sea,* at high tide, holding the hand of the gentleman known as the Inspector of Bathing, the town cannon was sounded!), did not own a bathing suit. She wore a jacket over a long woollen dress, an embroidered bonnet tied under the chin, and boots to protect her feet from the crabs.

Big Doll, the forebear of all the dolls, owned a pair of silk drawers with a matching camisole, white stockings and four outfits: white linen for summer, red velvet for late autumn, green striped taffeta for spring. Under my straw hat, which prevented her from seeing and breathing properly, she was wearing her brown winter skirt and a high-collared long-sleeved blouse. Doing up the tiny buttons on her blouse was a delicious occupation. Buttoning one by one the mother-of-pearl buttons of Big Doll's winter blouse gave me the same kind of pleasure as picking blackberries.

I knew a little girl, Marie, whose mother was a dressmaker. Her doll, Clara, had a wardrobe that was an exact replica of Marie's. When Marie went to the beach she laid Clara down on a square of towel the same colour as hers, the size of a face flannel. Then she lay down on her own towel, as relaxed as Clara on her scrap of fabric. Marie never wanted to run, play ball or swim. She didn't want to leave Clara. So Marie and Clara would lie there side by side, dressed identically and perfectly well behaved. The same smile on their lips.

One day I asked Marie if her mother had given Clara a swimming costume along with all her other outfits. She answered me, as if it were perfectly obvious, that no, her doll did not have a swimming costume. That was why she, Marie, never went in the water. But her mother had promised her an exact copy, in miniature, of the white dress she was going to wear for her first communion.

Marie was careful never to expose Clara to the sun. She had been brought up in the cult of pale skin. That left me perplexed, for shade, the worship of shade, of pallor as beauty, were values unknown in our house. Not because the opposite values had currency, but because of the absence of any system at all. My mother had no more respect for rules than she did for the traditions that upheld those values. At home even actions that were regularly and identically reproduced did not constitute any kind of routine or habit connecting one either to the past or to a project. Repeated actions did not constitute a lesson learnt. Every day, gestures and decisions were torn from virgin territory. It was not just because she couldn't bear groups, was resistant to teamwork and despised competition that my mother gave up the idea of actively seeking to become a champion swimmer. It was also the lack of a spirit of perseverance. There had been a stage when she was excited by the effort, during the endlessly open-ended period of youth. But leaving home meant relinquishing that boundless time when the whole world stretches out before you, glinting with multiple possibilities. The house at 14 Rue Nathaniel-Johnston closed off all those possibilities, leaving a single path open to her: to be a housewife. There was nothing attractive about this in her eyes, but instead of working out an escape route or trying to manipulate the situation to her advantage, she had this rigidity, a kind of stubborn obstinacy, that consisted of single-mindedly pursuing an outcome even when it was the worst possible. She ended up wanting nothing more for herself than to be a stay-at-home wife.

She was sitting – her body slightly twisted, perched on the edge of the chair as though she were about to get up (the same way she never lay on the beach, only sat there briefly, in passing) – at the garden table, a little heap of vegetables in front of her. She was wearing a yellow flowered two-piece and a sun hat. I sat next to her with a book in my lap. "Could you possibly imagine a more boring life?" she said to me, crying over the onions she was peeling.

Jackie decided to give up everything to do with sport. She gave up cycling, ping-pong, tennis and skiing. She never again mentioned the tandem that she had once dreamt of mounting with the adolescent boy who, because of a chain of circumstances that she could no longer recall, had become her husband. She could no longer envisage the two of them pedalling together in the same direction. From then on she did no sport apart from swimming, which she practised as a solitary rite, an act of survival, a manifesto of style.

We set off for the beach together. She undressed with her usual alacrity and headed towards the sea to test it with her toes. It was June. The water was still a little cold, just as she liked it. She turned to me with a look of joy.

Colette wrote about Sido, her mother, that she had two faces: her home face, sad, and her garden face, beaming. My mother, likewise, had two faces: her home face, sad, and her swimming face, radiant.

BATHING SUITS

I had only good relationships with my bathing suits. I can't say that was the case for all my clothes; skirts, especially, could be very awkward. They'd be too big around the waist, or too long. Or I'd have grown and they would have become ridiculously short. Whatever it was, it was annoying. Not to mention winter clothes: scarves, cardigans, pullovers and woolly hats that itch and smother you. Pointless, hostile clothes (I suspected that moving to Autumn Town meant more winter clothes). But do bathing suits count as clothing? That's a good question. Once upon a time, several summers earlier, going with or without a costume amounted to much the same thing. Even later, at an age when modesty was supposedly budding, it was still an exquisite pleasure after a swim to stand naked at the water's edge, rinsing the sand from my costume, watching it floating and sinking, then holding it in two fingers and wading farther out into the water, as if taking it for a walk. Even if in theory I'd finished my swim, the pretext of rinsing out my costume gave me an excuse to go back in the water. God alone knows how long the operation could last!

And then once I got home I loved hanging my costume out to dry, in the garden behind the house in the scent of the fig tree.

Simply saying or hearing someone say the word *bikini* was enough to make me swoon. If my mother was the queen of the swimming cap, I was born for the bikini.

My swimming costumes fitted my body perfectly. There was no constriction at all. There were a few I particularly loved, like my pink-and-white striped cotton bikini with a little triangular frill stitched onto the front. I could hold it scrunched up in one hand, no bigger than a handkerchief.

But more than anything else, what I loved secretly most of all was the evidence of the absent bikini at the end of summer, the whiteness of my buttocks, their luminous contrast with my brown skin.

THE TRIUMPH OF THE CRAWL

My mother was born on 16th September 1919, just after the end of the First World War, three months after the Treaty of Versailles was signed (on 28th June 1919, in the Hall of Mirrors in the Palace of Versailles, not far from their apartment on the Rue Sainte-Adélaïde). But I could also say that her history is not linked so much to the epic of the Nations but to that of swimming and, if one is to believe Paul Morand's extravagant panegyric, that she was born at the precise moment of the triumph of the crawl. In her fanatical and fixated devotion to this stroke, not only did she tirelessly explore the physical possibilities of the style, but she was in tune with one of the most superb athletic developments of her generation. "After 1918," writes Morand – himself an intrepid swimmer – in his book extolling the virtues of sea swimming, *Bains de mer*, "the crawl began to triumph, and it still reigns supreme. It took me a long time to learn to kick my feet in the rhythm of this marvellous stroke from Hawaii, at a time when it had yet to triumph at the Olympic games. [...] The crawl will remain for a long time, if not for all time, the most beautiful of all strokes. [...] The crawl is not only the fastest stroke but the one that reveals the human body in all its reptilian beauty. As with the gallop or the slalom, the harmony and balance begin in the hips; the arms and legs simply obey the helicoidal impulse that emanates from the waist, a movement that evolves and intensifies towards the extremities. The head is horizontal, controlled by taut, gleaming shoulders, and, in champions, by an impressive, chiselled musculature. Unlike diving, which is like swimming in the sky, the crawl is in harmony with the water; the swimmer, precise as a drill bit, moves along the aqueous surface, his body barely glimpsed out of the water, except for his heels and the wide angle of his elbows."

The writer goes into raptures about the *male* swimmer of the crawl – not the female. It is important to make clear that the female swimmer (of whatever stroke) was at this time a new and remarkable phenomenon in a history of humanity that has long been for women a history of immobilization, of an imposed, and largely accepted, designation as modest and frail beings, delicate creatures who had to remain on the shore bundled up in petticoats, dresses and shawls, protected from the wind and the sun. That was when they were lucky enough to be allowed to leave the house and go anywhere near the water – which they were only authorized to do because they had to watch over the children. The women would sit together, covered from head to foot, eyes never straying from their progeny. As for undressing and entering the water, getting wet, swimming towards the horizon, being submerged in the water's calm embrace, forgetting everything that came before: this victory took centuries. It is far from complete.

Paul Morand admits that he never learnt to swim the crawl well. He managed the kick and the movement of the arms, but he failed to master the breathing. He would practise, his face submerged in a bowl, his mouth twisted and his uvula closed; it's not working! I never managed more than a few metres either before I was out of breath. I could hear my mother's voice as she stood in the water, urging me to find the right breathing rhythm. I'd be all over the place, splashing everywhere, swallowing water, going under, my eyes burning. I hated that she wanted to teach me the crawl. I was used to feeling in perfect harmony with the water, but now it had become an element apart, almost foreign. My mother had absolutely no educational instincts whatsoever, except when it came to teaching me the crawl. Then she was unrelenting, like those parents who force you to eat up or do your homework during the holidays. But her drive came up against my resistance, and revealed something about it. Now our days at the beach began with her teaching me the crawl. I preferred to let myself sink. My mother moved away, or I did.

She continued her marvellous aquatic crawling, while I insisted on paddling. She tried to inculcate in me a sense of pace and direction. She treated me as if I didn't know how to swim, whereas as far as I was concerned – and this was a fundamental conviction – I knew how to swim, *I had always known how to swim*. Tumbling in the waves is swimming. No, she said, and added, "Go ahead and do your doggy-paddle, if you think it's fun. When everyone laughs at you, that'll be your problem. I don't have the patience. Patience infuriates me."

She pulled on her swimming cap covered in daisies. I loved her daisy-cap. With a dancer's grace, she poked in some loose strands of hair and swam away. I watched her. I was sitting half in the water, half in the sun, on that elusive boundary where the water meets the shore. I was about to cry. Very quietly, just for me. But just then a bigger wave surged and tipped me over in the foam. I tumbled in an endless prism of light and water.

When she returned, transformed as always by her swim, she was calm and smiling. She handed me her daisy-cap as if it were a bouquet of flowers. I played my fingers over it, fiddling with the petals that I couldn't pluck off. One morning, because of that swimming cap and my love for the flowers that adorned it, she told me her middle name: Marguerite.

With her gift for inconstancy, Jackie-Marguerite bore no grudge over the disastrous lesson. She wasn't angry with me for refusing to do the crawl. Well, perhaps a little, which was why she kept trying to teach me the "marvellous crawl", to show me its "reptilian beauty".

But for now she was serene and relaxed, watching me doing forward rolls on the noonday sand. When I got up and stumbled, a little dizzy, my hair full of sand, she asked me, "Do you like this beach?"

FLOATING

I didn't need to learn the crawl, or any other stroke, because *I already knew how to swim.* I couldn't explain, it was just how it was. All it took, after I'd amused myself for a while one day in the tide pools, was crossing the sandbars to get to the bay – the sea, in other words – where I lay down in the little wavelets, then, quite simply, let myself be carried off…

I was surrounded by fine strands of floating kelp, not brown and coiled like the tassels of dried kelp amassed on the sand like knots of hair, but sinuous ribbons of drifting sea grass, in soft, burnished green. Beneath their gentle undulations little crabs scurried back and forth. When I stopped swimming and put my feet down to walk they tickled my toes.

My mother swam from one jetty to the next, while I meandered among the boats, hanging on to the buoys. It was impossible to mark out my route, even less to establish my speed. Impossible to put a number on my "performance". My mother thought the way I swam was slapdash. Sportingly indefensible. She simply didn't believe in it.

That last summer we lived with my grandparents my best friend was a little boy from Paris who also – according to the criteria in force at the time – couldn't swim. He was just pretending to, his family would tease him. We were doing the walk-float together quite happily one day, when all of a sudden he began to drift. I saw his look of horror as the current dragged him away. He didn't shout; it was I who screamed. His father raced into the water and managed to save him. He was half-drowned. They rubbed him vigorously up and down until he was full of vim again; I heard him murmur proudly, in spite of his terror: "It was amazing, did you see how far I swam?"

There really is such a thing as the walk-float, just as opera has its *Sprechgesang*, its musical declamation. But in order to appreciate it one needs a highly refined, I'd go so far as to say microscopic, sense of nuance.

I learnt to swim by playing. Like a sea turtle, I progressed effortlessly from sunbathing to seabathing, happy simply to hold my neck higher out of the water. I didn't experience this as a jump up to the next level, but as an increasingly dependable weightlessness, a total trust in the water, a trust inseparable from the feeling of love. Whenever I heard my parents say, "It's crazy how much she loves the water," the sheer essence of the word *love* resounded in my ears and my heart. The water was my love. And in the expression "the water is perfect", I intuited a reference not only to temperature but also to a moral essence.

The bay is goodness to me.

I lie on my back, unmoving, arms outstretched. I float on my back, my eyes open to the sky. I lie, relaxed, on the water, as one might lie on a boat.

THE FISHERIES BEACH

Yes, I did like this new beach. It stretched from the Eyrac jetty to Aiguillon Point and the port. Depending on the day we would find a spot either near the jetty or closer to Aiguillon. Usually we chose somewhere in the middle, near the fisheries buildings. I called it the "fishing beach". It was bordered with villas that, seen from the sea at high tide, appeared to float (arriving by boat from Cap Ferret it always looked to me as though the whole town were afloat). Farther along towards the port the villas gave way to the fisheries buildings and boatyards, where people used to service and repair fishing smacks and trawlers, and make nets.

The very word *fisheries*, and the site itself – its stalls glistening with mullet, bream, stone bass, conger eels, gurnard, black sea bream, turbot, skate, monkfish, sea bass – enchanted me. The fish gleaming silver-grey, blue, bronze, sometimes enhanced with specks of orange, red dots, yellow stripes. Lying on a bed of ice, the fish exposed to the light something of the bay's depths, a hint of the ocean's violence. But their dead eyes, open to nothing, protected their mystery. This new beach connected me to another universe, showed me a different relationship with the sea: the world of sailors, the wisdom of fishermen, the danger of storms. It revealed something of the vastness and depths of the ocean. It defied reasonable limits.

The beach down by the Thiers jetty, which I had been going to since I was born, the beach where I used to go in my tiny Noah's Ark, is for holidaymakers. It's associated in my mind with bandstand music, ice cream and waffle stalls, the carousel, ladies and gentlemen strolling, taking breaks on a bench, sitting for hours looking at the sea, the comings and goings of the fishing smacks, the Isle of Birds as it appeared and disappeared. A genteel beach for people like me and my little seaside friends. People of leisure rediscovering a child's sense of the fluidity of time, with less frenzy.

These holidaymakers never went down to the fisheries beach; parasols were a rare sight there. Children would meet up there in packs, tight and lasting. We played there all the time, whether it was actually the holidays or not. The new beach was vast: we ran and ran, on and on. That was our game at low tide. We ran, as fast as we could, elbows tucked in, heels slapping the hard sand. The grown-ups watched us as we passed. "Where are they running to?" they would ask, before looking back down at their crossword puzzles. We ran. We were galloping horses, slaves escaping from the plantations, convicts on the loose. The space was wide open ahead of us. We ran. The sheer watery surface exploded in sparks as our feet struck the sand.

Nothing and no one could overtake us, except the shadows of the clouds as they raced over the earth.

In truth, I never really moved away. Either to a new house or a new beach. I regularly went back to Avenue Régnault and to the beach by the Thiers jetty. The new house and the new beach didn't erase those that preceded them. Just as Saint-Ferdinand, the church in Autumn Town, in the heart of the old port neighbourhood, co-existed with the Basilica of Our Lady, farther along from the Sailors' jetty.

GETTING INTO THE WATER

We children were always laughing as we got into the water, splashing and pushing each other over. Getting into the water wasn't a decisive act for us. The water had no threshold. The grown-ups did it completely differently: you could see it in the way they hesitated, in the way they kept stopping, in their habits: splashing a bit of water on their neck, making circles with their hands, as if they were trying to discern their degree of sensitivity to the cold, or as if they were stopping themselves from walking back to their beach towels by repeatedly rotating their hands. Most would get into the sea millimetre by millimetre, moving more and more slowly as the water reached their sensitive parts. A sensitivity to cold is particular to grown-ups. Splash them with a few drops of water at that moment and you'd find out how hysterical they really were. Right in front of everybody they'd explode and start yelling.

Getting into the water was a real saga for the grown-ups, the women in particular. Some spent more time getting in than they did swimming. They would no doubt have responded that the difficulty with us was getting out of the water. In reality that was completely different. We would drag it out, beg – five more minutes, three minutes, one minute! – but that was to make the pleasure last as long as possible. By dint of our parents' repeated calls, and our unsuccessful pleas, we would eventually get out. Sometimes we took so long that by the time we were out we were trembling with cold. Our teeth were chattering, the tips of our fingers were wrinkled, and nothing would warm us up, no matter how hard we rubbed ourselves with towels and layered on dry clothes. We didn't care. If we could have we would have gone straight back into the water, notwithstanding the cold and shivering, to continue our games.

Our parents fished us out, blue and shivering, and those who still had the strength would stammer *no*, they didn't want to get out. Their parents had better stop trotting out that promise that was supposed to placate our watery obsession, those empty words: *You'll be back tomorrow.*

Tomorrow doesn't exist.

We were blue with cold, but all we cared about was the cruel bite of the present.

My mother didn't enter the water like the fashionable ladies who didn't want to get their permanent waves wet, or those snooty, yelping women always trying to seem interesting. ("Be brave, madame! Once you start swimming, you'll find the water is perfect!") My mother would go in up to her waist, wait very briefly, then plunge in. At the end of her swim, the same straight back and economy of movement. She would flip over and do a few metres of backstroke to return to the shore. Actually, it was rare to see my mother getting out of the water. I usually saw her walking back along the beach after she'd swum her chosen distance for the day. She would be looking pleased with herself, relaxed (in spite of having just expended real physical effort), walking towards me, towards my beach towel spread out on the sand, my bag filled with sand blown in on the breeze, my fishing net. I'd be lying on my tummy, drowsy with well-being and warmth. My mother would sit down, back straight, like a lookout, on a small towel (she used her towel to sit on; the idea of stretching out on a beach towel was completely alien to her), her face and body aglow, staring out to sea. My mother never rested, never lounged – except on the sea.

Getting into the water was always done in silence. She despised those shriekers who would take a long run up on the sand and then rush headlong into the water, speeding up before diving in with a yell. What brutes, attacking the water, provoking it, as if it were a rival. Mad dogs. Show-offs! The same men who liked nothing more than, with a friend, picking a girl up by her arms and legs, dragging her to the water's edge, and throwing her in.

My mother never deigned to give those types a single glance.

At home, my father organized a corner of the garage into a workshop. This allowed him to hole up on his own. This was where he was happy. He also spent as much time as he could on his boat. He never came to the beach with us. He might stop to wave as he passed, before setting off on the boat. I never saw him in the water either. He would dive from the boat, letting himself slip behind it, and swim in the wake. I could hear the muffled splash as he fell.

THE LESSON FAMILY

It wasn't only seaweed and shellfish that mesmerized me. Humankind also offered up some fascinating specimens. I would observe them as closely as the other mysteries of the seashore, with exactly the same attention. I'd like to have been able to pick them up and manipulate them like the marionettes I had at home, but since they were human beings, and not seaweed or shellfish, I learnt to employ a certain discretion in my behaviour. They didn't realize they were being watched, and I soon discovered that my observations were not compromised as a result of my discretion.

The Lesson family lived in a white villa with peeling white shutters. A big, old villa with a veranda, a turret and a large garden. The villa was right on the water. I was very envious of the turret and the veranda, but not nearly as much as I was of the stone staircase leading down to the beach that dropped at high tide straight into the sea, so that the Lesson children could make their way step by step down the marvellous stairway directly into the water. If they were allowed to. But in the Lesson family permission was rarely granted. There were five children, all quite ugly, like their parents. So it was not physical beauty that drew me to them. But there was something else, something alien to me. My mother's mood swings created a climate of instability where at any moment a situation might be overturned and plans changed. The Lesson family seemed by contrast to be ferociously serious. They did everything *quite properly*.

I loved watching them have their breakfast outside on the terrace, all clean and perfectly ironed. Next they would do their holiday homework, and only then, just before noon, were they allowed a swim as their reward. If one of the children had been punished he was not allowed to go swimming. On top of that the child might have to suffer an *explanation*. That was the part I liked best: the two characters, mother and child, walking back and forth along the shore. Fully dressed, of course (rolled up trousers, skirt hitched up to the knees). The mother reeling off her monotonous lecture. The child listening, head hanging. It might last a very long time. I'd be paddling in the shallows, catching snatches of her words. I would hear: *naughty, responsibility, future, your brothers and sisters, term time*… I'd plunge my head under water and then emerge to hear a terrible phrase scold the child like a slap: *boarding school*. The word *father* was rarely uttered. By and large, Papa Lesson did not get involved. He would sit in a rattan armchair and smoke his pipe. He always had a book or a newspaper in his hand. He emanated an elegant sense of ennui. And, whenever necessary, he had an unfaltering aptitude for saying *no* to his children's assorted demands, so that the maternal counsel *Ask your father* ended up being understood as a *no* that simply had yet to be formulated. It was the father's role to articulate the refusal. He dealt it out in a neutral tone, with no evident reluctance. He never attempted to break out of the superior sphere in which he sat and brooded. The wife was more down to earth. Perhaps because of her short, stocky legs.

But even when their mood matched the fine weather and the family was relaxing – they might be playing croquet, laughing about some silly thing the littlest one had done, reading a story aloud to the children – the parents never stopped talking like parents, their voices always a touch too loud. Was that to make the question "Did you hear what I just said?" sound more accusatory, or was it because the whole family suffered from a congenital hearing problem? Were the Lesson children all born with silted-up lugholes? It wouldn't have mattered if they were, since the family clearly had no fear of endless repetition.

Mama Lesson had a detestable habit: she would give an order and then say, "Careful now! I'm going to count to three." And then she would count, very distinctly, the time allotted for the implementation of the task. She would enunciate very slowly: "One, two, three..." And if, by the count of three, the child had not obeyed, it would get a slap.

The Lesson family – and this comes as no surprise – were acquaintances of the Digit family.

There were several villas neighbouring the house occupied by the Lesson family. They were all built facing the sea, with large gardens, were completely dead during the winter and came alive in the summer – and they all displayed the same highly regulated family life, the same hum of self-satisfaction that is passed down, almost unaltered, from generation to generation, along with the inheritance of the villa. They were my first experience of theatre – the performance of adult life, the representation of a structured family – and, without my even being conscious of it, the distance from which I observed them would prevent me later on from ever passing over to their side, as if there was always a strip of sand between them and me, like a buffer zone.

When we played the card game Happy Families, I would ask, in exchange for any Digit or Lesson, for Mama Mercurial, Grandpa Railway, or Papa Silence. I would ask for what I already had.

METAMORPHOSES

I may have wondered if it was actually worth learning to walk, given that crawling on all fours was just as efficient and much more fun. Having finally opted for the passage to the vertical position, I had every reason to congratulate myself, all the more so as, among its numerous advantages, it did not require renouncing the low-lying landscape of the sand and its microscopic marvels, that peerless proximity when we find ourselves, awestruck, looking at "the crimson crenellated spire of some seashell, tapering to a turret and glazed with enamel" (Proust). To my eyes, the treasures of the sea will always more than measure up to the achievements of those who build cathedrals.

Some years later (how many? I have no idea), I entertained serious doubts about the usefulness of learning to count. Why would I inflict such an onerous task on myself when, as Félix never stopped reminding me, to live on the bay was to inhabit a world impossible to measure? (The Digit family was distinctly out of place in this part of the world.) The ocean floor here cannot be gauged. It eludes any attempt at calculable localization, cannot be described in detail on any map. For a long time, Arcachon Bay, the only breach along the whole of the Gascony coast, was highly dangerous for sailors to approach. They had to cross the sound without running aground on the sandbanks; their mute terror ringing out louder than the din of the waves, they did their best to navigate in such a way as to avoid the ghastly crunch of the hull against the ocean floor. "The sea has touched the bottom!" the sailors would cry. None of them could swim. The ship was already taking on water as they prayed to the Virgin of the Shipwrecks to save them. They drowned intoning their very last prayer, to Mary, to their mother.

The sandbanks are impossible to pinpoint. Even the perimeter of the bay, like the living frill of an oyster's cape, changes all the time. I inhabited – was growing up in – a universe in flux. Everything in and around the bay was constantly shifting. On the shore, the alluvial sands that came in from the sea; inland, the living sands of the dune.

On the beach, I never repeated the exact same route down to the water. I zigzagged between parasols, waves and dinghies. I delighted in the amethyst hue of a shell picked up in the shallows. By the time it dried it had lost its lustre and changed colour.

The route down to the water's edge varied according to the tides, yes, but also according to my mood, my curiosity and a host of diverse lures, both people and things. Some were recurrent, like the cuttlefish bones, their pallor, their lightness, their shape somewhere between an oval and an ogive. They were like a kind of flat, salted meringue. Everything picked up on the beach is salted, something I liked to verify with a flick of the tongue. The same applied to everything that came out of the water, including my own body after a swim.

Still dripping, I would hug my upper arm to drink the salt.

The way back up the beach was also part of the perpetual flux of the world around me.

I wasn't growing up: I was changing.

LUCILE

The children of families strategically organized to endure and prosper stick together. They are not allowed to play with strangers. The beach, like the road, is a public place and, consequently, threatening. As it happens, though I was naturally sociable, I had no desire to play with a little Lesson or borrow a ball from one of the young Digits. I didn't need company. I never have. When I was little it was because I was self-contained (or put another way, I never left the house without several dolls); later, because the beach made meeting people so easy. We coexisted in a fragile world. We might play together for an hour, a morning, or an entire summer. We didn't bother each other with questions. If a child was summoned by her parents and came to tell us, sadly, that it was all over, it was the last day of the holidays, we would be sad too; we would briefly interrupt our game and our high spirits would subside. But as soon as she left new friends arrived to take her place, and we would start again with the same zeal. We carried on building sandcastles and watching them crumble, digging holes, burying a more or less consenting victim under shovelfuls of sand. Our victim, docile to begin with, would suddenly leap up out of his tomb; covered in sand, like ashes, he would race away and dive into the sea. My beach friends were endlessly replaceable. There was always a new victim to be found, and the transformation of victim into persecutor took place in no time at all.

The day I met Lucile for the first time the wind was up. The roiling waves were embossed with tiny kinks, and the surface of the tide pools – small lakes with a channel that carves through the sand to join the sea, child-sized swimming holes – shivered. My mother hated the wind. It was not yet the absolute enemy that it would become a few years later, but it was no longer the light breeze of her first summers in Arcachon, nor the lively gusts of the period when she used to walk me up and down the Boulevard de la Plage, when she enjoyed stooping into the wind as she tried to outflank it. By now, she certainly no longer considered it an equal partner. She looked with loathing at the water she wouldn't be able to swim in because of the wind. She tried to knit. The wind blew sand in her eyes. If there were no wind she could knit undisturbed, but, bearing in mind that she hated knitting no less than the wind, I didn't see what she stood to gain. She knotted a scarf around her hair and wanted to do the same to mine. I wasn't sure – I liked the feeling of my hair whipping around my head like the dried grass on the dunes. My mother went back to her knitting. "It's *infuriating*! A day like today I might just as well have stayed in bed!" I moved beyond the radius of her frayed nerves and started walking towards the water. My route to happenstance. The tide was out.

I walked until I came across a little girl kneeling in a tide pool. She had fished out a starfish that she was holding in the palm of her hand. I crouched down to her level to admire her catch: it was gorgeous, raspberry pink and very delicate. "Here!" she said, placing it in my hand. I felt something both abrasive and soft. The little girl leant towards me and whispered in my ear: "Look after it. It's a gift from the Princess of the Palace of the Sea." Her face was narrow, with dark eyes that shone so brightly I couldn't make out their colour, and black hair cut straight in a bob that rippled in the wind. Her fringe grazed my cheek. I dared not accept such a gift. I tried to hand it back to the little girl but she stopped me. "It belongs to you now," she said. I sensed that I was going to have to keep it. But I was worried. What if it really was a royal gift?

"The princess, won't she be angry? Does she get cross easily?"

"Sometimes."

"Take it back then."

"No, it belongs to you now."

On a day when my mother was already in a bad mood, I didn't need a princess on my back as well.

"But you said it was a present from a princess..."

"Yes, the Princess of the Palace of the Sea."

"You can't give it away to just anybody."

"You aren't just anybody."

I was touched by what she said. The little girl whispered something else. (She had an affecting whisper, nothing like the gruff whisper of the confessor.) I hung on her every word.

Just then we heard our mothers calling our names. "Lucile! Chantal! Lucile! Chantal!" Curiously, they were both calling us at the same time, as if they realized before we did that we were about to become inseparable and that from now on they would have to negotiate with one child divided in two, or two children speaking as one, but never again with their supposed only child. The muffled sound of their voices reached us on the sea breeze, almost inaudible against the sound of the surf. Instead of obeying we ran in the opposite direction to swim. Quickly, because our mothers were insisting; their voices might be weak, but their hold on us was real. My hand closed over the starfish. I decided to dry it and paint it with a layer of varnish, like I did with seahorses.

THE LORD OF THE DUNES

I didn't know anything about my friend with the starfish. All we knew about each other was our names. I didn't even know if she would come back to the beach, or if she was just a day-tripper. For once, I really cared. For once, tomorrow existed. I got up and checked the sky. It was overcast. It was going to rain. No beach today. I was not going to see her again. I had a horrible day that was made even more unpleasant by my mother's reaction to my display of starfish and seahorses, laid out to dry on a low wall (it's true that it was very near the kitchen). "What an awful smell!" she said in her clear, lovely voice. "Take your little trinkets somewhere else, please, or I'm throwing them in the bin." I rushed to do it. Terrible, the idea that the royal treasure might go in the rubbish! I gathered up my collection and spread it out as far away as possible. The bottom of the garden was shaded by the fig tree, whose perfume aroused something strange in me. Because the fig tree was itself in the shadow of the neighbouring house, its fruits never ripened. I picked a still-green fig, not to eat it, just to see the milky liquid trickle out and smear my fingers. The smell of my collection didn't overpower the perfume of the fig tree.

The following day the sun was shining and – oh joy! – Lucile was already at the beach by the time I arrived. Her mother, having plastered herself with it from head to toe, was now rubbing sun cream on her daughter. Lucile waved. The minute her mother finished she rushed over. We needed an isolated spot away from ears and unwelcome intrusions so that she could tell me more. Since we couldn't find one we were going to have to make it ourselves. We needed a wall, so that we could be invisible and inaudible to the rest of the beach. It turns out it takes a long time to build a wall out of sand; it's never high enough and every time it reaches a certain height it collapses. Eventually we gave up and contented ourselves with huddling behind a fishing boat. Lucile took up the thread of the conversation as though she had spent the whole of the previous day reflecting on the question, or had just that moment come out of an interview with Her.

"The princess isn't mean. I think she's nice really. But she has a bad temper. People say horrid things about her, you've probably heard them."

I shook my head. At home we listened to *chansons* on the wireless and my mother had no interest in other people's lives. Lucile was astonished. Her mother was obsessed with other people's lives. She always had a book in her hand. All she did was read about other people, read and teach about other people's lives, because she taught literature ("*Everybody*'s lives?" "Yes, *everybody*'s lives." I asked the question purely as a matter of form, for her mother's job did not interest me in the slightest). Eventually Lucile returned to the subject. "The princess doesn't have a good reputation, it's true," she said, "but she has an excuse..." We were crouched down side by side behind the fishing smack. A gorgeous morning stretched out ahead of us.

Lucile launched into her saga; her voice was soft and low and she had the air of someone both terrified and excited by the massive secret she was about to impart... "A long time ago," she whispered, "a very long time ago, at the very, very beginning, the Sand and the Sea were at war. The princess's father, the Lord of the Dunes, was a Giant. All the sand belonged to him, but it was never enough. He positioned armed guards along the coast to keep watch over his sand, so that not a single grain could escape to join the Sea. He had a daughter, a little girl whom he treated terribly. He stopped her from growing by keeping her prisoner under sacks of sand. But one day she managed to escape, this tiny girl, flat and deformed from the heavy weights that had been pressing down on her since she was born. She hid in the forest. She could hardly see because sand fleas had eaten her eyes. She guided herself by the patches of green moss and resin-scented ferns. She was so flat that she easily slipped between the planks of the resin tappers' huts. She could go in and out without being seen. She was trying to escape from the forest so she could reach the Sea, but the Lord of the Dunes controlled the forest. In his fury he buried everything under torrents of sand that he rained down on the resin tappers. The poor little misshapen girl, half-blind, unable to find her bearings, kept bumping into her Giant father's feet. Whether she followed the paths or the gullies, it made no difference. She ran, panic-stricken, skidding on pine needles, stumbling over roots, gashed by brambles. Her father watched her run for a little while, for his amusement, then he closed his enormous hand around her and imprisoned her once more. Each time the fate of the poor princess was even more terrible. Finally he chained her to a wall, where she was condemned to end her days."

As Lucile told the story it unfolded before her eyes. Before *our* eyes. We lost all awareness of time. We couldn't move.

There she was, right in front of us, the little princess, the daughter of the Lord of the Dunes, the scapegoat of the General of the Sands. She really was very small, quite shrunken, with brown hair and sad, dark eyes, her lashes white as sand, her fringe bleached too. Lucile stopped talking. We were in a trance. And then all of a sudden we realized that the tide had come in. It had almost reached the marooned boat that we were using as a screen. I shook myself awake and pulled Lucile up with me.

We looked up and down the beach, now almost completely covered by the rising waters. I asked her:

"Back then, right at the very, very beginning, when the Sand and the Sea were enemies, what was at the bottom of the water?"

"At the bottom of the water, there was water. It was like today with air. At the bottom of the air there's air."

"But now the water has a floor. There's sand and silt."

"I know," she said, a little impatient.

"And there's green seaweed growing on the bottom, with long stalks. The floor of the bay is like a huge meadow."

"Really?"

It was her turn to be astonished. I was pleased to regain a little of my superiority as a child of the shore.

"All that kelp, have you never wondered where it comes from? It comes from the seaweed. On the beach it's all dried up."

"Like hay?"

"Exactly."

We took armfuls of kelp to make pillows. The air beneath the midday sun was burning hot. We lay down and closed our eyes and imagined ourselves walking together in the watery green of the underwater meadow.

THE PRINCESS OF THE PALACE OF THE SEA

We decided we didn't need a hide, we just had to talk very quietly. In truth, it was impossible to keep out of sight of our mothers and my former playmates. They too had noticed, as our mothers had, that they had been spurned in one fell swoop by our new bond. Every once in a while, great wafts of jealousy were carried to me on the breeze, along with the odour of iodine and seaweed. Only I was aware of this: my new friend was blessed with the obliviousness of a newcomer. Life at the beach began with her arrival, and, as the repository of the saga of the Princess of the Palace of the Sea and the obligation to share it with someone, she was completely impervious to the spiteful signals being sent out by my abandoned friends.

In a low voice, staring straight ahead, Lucile spoke. "This time, with chains fixing her to the wall and binding her ankles, she had no chance of escape. The princess was wasting away. She spat out the disgustingly gritty rations served to her by the Lord of the Dunes."

"Like what?"

"Um... rind of pig fat rolled in black sand, stuffed spine of sea urchin, braised shoe leather, strangled doves, rotted goose stew, grated rabbit brain... Her only hope was that she would become so skeletal that the chains would loosen and no longer hold her. But she was under close guard by her torturers who were themselves being terrorized by the Lord of the Dunes. Her resistance was almost completely worn away, and she decided to let herself die. But, one scorching hot August night, when she had given up all hope, her father suddenly flew into a terrifyingly violent rage. His explosion of fury cracked the Dune and made a huge chunk of his empire crumble into the Sea. When he saw this disaster his fury intensified, and another chunk of his empire, where his luckless daughter was imprisoned, sheered off. Holding on tight with her skinny arms to the slab of hardened sand that had been the floor of her prison, she was flung far over the Ocean. A flying trip, a swooping arc over the waves. Light as a feather she landed on the water, drifting on her sandy raft. Other slabs of sand, flung clear of the tyrant's domain, massed around her, wide enough to make a foundation for her palace and a floor for the bay.

"Sand and Sea were reconciled. The little princess, cleansed of muck and fear, gave up her repulsive diet for delicious oysters and became very pretty – and powerful too, for thanks to her armada of moving sandbanks, the scourge of cartographers and bane of sailors, she was able to wreck ships whenever she wanted."

And that is how the Princess of the Palace of the Sea became a formidable shipwrecker, *the* shipwrecker of the bay. I thought about Our Lady of Arcachon, the statue saved from a shipwreck by brother Thomas Illyricus. Was it the Princess of the Palace of the Sea who was responsible for the shipwreck that almost led to Mary's drowning? Had she been witness to it? The monk on his knees, praying on the shore, the huge waves, the exceptional violence of the wind and the rain; and then, during a miraculous lull, Mary emerging from the waves, her crown still firmly on her head, eyes unblinking, her one unbroken arm cradling her baby. The monk waded into the sea and fished out the mother and her inanimate child. Helped by the mother he resuscitated the child and then wrapped them both in a blanket. As soon as the child was out of danger, he hastily built a wooden shack, away from the waves, where the dunes began. He made it out of lengths of pine, covered the roof with gorse and spread a generous layer of pine needles over the floor. He gazed upon them both, the young woman, barely older than a child, and her son, Jesus. He knelt and declaimed: *Ave Maria, gratia plena, Dominus tecum. Benedicta tu in mulieribus, et benedictus fructus ventris tui, Iesus!*

He would look for flowers tomorrow, wild carnations.

This was the first chapel to be erected in Arcachon, and for Thomas Illyricus – as he strode across the marshes, consumed by despair as he tried to understand what he was doing there, why he had been condemned to this wasteland at the ends of the earth, why he, Orator, Preacher, spewer of righteous anger, known to ecstatic crowds as "He Who Proclaims the Word of God", had inflicted on himself the worst torment of all, solitude – for Brother Thomas, tortured hermit, this was his first moment of peace.

From the depths of her palace, its gaping entrance screened by the swaying weeds of the sea, the princess must surely have witnessed the scene. Though she loved the spectacle of shipwrecks, the ear-splitting screams and bursts of flame, she hated the melancholy desolation that inevitably followed. So she rejoiced that this time – just as it had been for her – disaster had given birth to a miracle.

I kept my musings to myself. I didn't want to interrupt the beautiful story that my friend was telling me with the same self-possession as when she gave me the starfish. And anyway, as far as I could judge, it appeared that over the countless years since the dramatic rescue of Mary and her child, there had never been the slightest conflict between the Princess of the Palace of the Sea and She who would go on to be celebrated as (among other names) Our Lady of the Sea. Quite the contrary, indeed. After the original chapel erected in Mary's honour – the shack fashioned from branches and flowers – was buried beneath the sands and battered by the tides, another chapel, larger, solid and dry, was built. The first chapel, now an underwater ruin, was incorporated into the palace furnishings. The princess displayed her multi-coloured collection of anemone jewellery on a table top that had once been the chapel roof. And, meanwhile, what became of the monk? I needed to ask my grandfather, for it was he who had told me this story. It was our secret, just as the princess was a secret that belonged to Lucile and me, and they must not be confused.

Lucile introduced me to the secrets of the Princess of the Palace of the Sea, and I shared with her my twin predilections for collecting treasures at low tide and the close observation of human specimens. She preferred the former by far. While she quickly learnt to spot the subtle darting concealment of shrimp, crabs and other creatures during the hours of low tide, and was full of admiration for their camouflage techniques, she found the Theatre of Family Life extremely dull.

"But nothing ever happens," she said to me one day after several mornings spent observing the comings and goings of the Lesson family.

"That's what's so fabulous. They do everything properly, and always the same way."

She looked at me without understanding. She didn't grasp what was so extraordinary about it. Perhaps quite simply because that was how it was for her at home. Whatever it was, she preferred to examine the villas before their inhabitants arrived. To penetrate walls, peer under water, graze the invisible that vibrates within. She had a gift for the concealed.

IN THE SHADOW OF THE RUSTED JETTY

We kept the sphere of our intrigues closed to the outside world. Out of reverence for our cult of secrecy, but also out of necessity – it was simply impossible to translate the consuming experiences of our days into understandable words. We lived and breathed a kind of constant rapture, a thousand things took place, but by evening we had nothing to tell. When someone asked, "Did you have fun today?" we simply answered, "Yes," with a slightly weary expression. The term *have fun* seemed so awkward, a terribly frivolous way of describing the intensity with which we explored our ephemeral constructions of sand and water, scrutinized their very impermanence. There was something in the nature of our activities, some indescribable quality, which reduced us to silence. We did not communicate anything, because there was nothing about our activities that could be communicated.

This was especially true after we had spent hours paddling around the pillars of the rusted jetty on our beach. It wasn't a pier for holidaymakers, like those on the Chapelle, Thiers and Eyrac beaches, but a wharf built for the shipyards and canning factories. Like that other Arcachon, the Arcachon that had long been in decline, peopled by those who worked on the sea, who went fishing as far as Newfoundland and Iceland, the Arcachon of peril and poverty that had already been almost entirely supplanted by tourism, the jetty used by industry and commerce was as good as inoperative. We thought of it as already abandoned, although there were two cranes fixed to either end of it that were still in use. In the shadow of the jetty the water was frigid and almost black, illuminated only by a few rays of light that filtered through the pierced bulkhead. Exploring in this absence of light filled us with a mixture of dread and jubilation. But jubilation won out as we moved closer to the pillars to peer at the strange conglomerate, completely encrusted with seashells and soft patches of green algae. The rust fascinated us, an intrusion of industry into the landscape where we swam. I was gripped by the same fascination as when I went to Aiguillon port in the early morning when the fishermen were unloading their cargo. Just as much as the fish on the bridge (some still thrashing in the tangle of nets), the trawlers themselves were fabulous – haloed, whatever the weather, by the aura of storms, and chained to their enormous anchors.

The rust-covered pillars signalled to us not only the existence of the world of work but, more importantly, the existence of time. If we knew almost nothing of the world of work, we knew even less of time. Every day at the beach, every blazing morning, began with the erasure of the day before. But however hard the pillars tried, like Big Doll keeping vigil in the wardrobe in my bedroom, holding in the glassy reflection of her huge, sleeping eyes images of my great-grandmother Zélie as a little girl, it was a waste of effort. We were conscious only of the water lapping against our thighs, a ferruginous sensation beneath our fingers. We tried to pull off some mussels, tugged at colonies of pointy limpets, only giving up as the tide began to come in. Then we would abandon our haunt of shadows and encrustations, swimming away as fast as we could, suddenly afraid of this carcass planted in the sea, afraid that we might have been scratched by a shard of twisted metal and that the deadly tetanus microbe had already infused our blood.

Or – and with no less conviction – we might choose the curative virtues of ferruginous water and stay floating even longer in the water, letting the invisible red particles transmit their strength to us.

In the shadow of the rusted jetty sometimes we risked being trapped by death, sometimes we pursued the benefits of an iron constitution. These sudden turnarounds and contradictory changes did not bother us. They were intrinsic to our understanding of the water, which, from swim to swim, or while we gazed at the sea from a distance – or even when we couldn't see it, when we were walking down an alleyway, say, and a gust of saline air caressed our cheeks – was growing in us.

We never tried to talk about the emotions triggered by the rust, any more than we would ever share how much we loved the muddy silt, that delicious, smooth as velvet, delicately squelching substance that we loved to sink into. We didn't ask for wooden boards to strap onto our shoes to walk over it. On the mudflats we would extend our legs as far as we could, taking giant strides so that we could place our feet into the prints hollowed out by my father. And we sang hymns of praise to the Mud Sprite, who abolished angles and sculpted our bodies in relief, like an embrace.

SEA GLEANERS

It was high summer, the exploration of a new beach, the discovery of inseparable friendship. Lucile was in Arcachon for the whole of the holidays, in other words for eternity. I was never worried when I said goodbye to her at the end of the day. Every evening the ceremony of our farewells was interminable, a performance of tragedy every bit as dramatic as the drift of our days was tranquil.

Lucile and I did everything together. We tried to have our parents buy the same clothes for us, swimming costumes, shorts, striped sweaters, the same colour jelly shoes, the same straw hats.

We loved low tide. The beach became huge. We could walk almost all the way to the Isle of Birds.

We had our own language. We swam bizarrely. We didn't believe the world obeyed the laws of physics but that it was tamed by magic. From the outside we must have seemed uncoordinated, because our impulses were so unpredictable. In reality, everything we did was remarkably thought through, and we were absolutely focused on every single one of our undertakings.

I admit that it must have been difficult to see this: our challenges meant nothing to anyone but us, and we valued above all the cult of the secret.

Our mothers frequently lost sight of us, and we of them.

We were the sea gleaners, foragers of kelp, bards of the princess. We kept going straight ahead, never looking back.

DIVING

Our mothers didn't have much to say to each other. If it hadn't been for us they would have had no reason to spend any time together at all. But we existed and our secretive, distant behaviour, our endless whispering, our jittery impatience whenever we were apart, was beginning to get on both their nerves. As well as the way we wandered off far down the beach towards Aiguillon, spent our days in the shadow of the rusted jetty, and the snippets of conversation that they managed to catch without us noticing – those stories about the palace at the bottom of the sea, and the princess who rose up against the Lord of the Dunes – which caused them to raise their eyes to the heavens, beg God to give them strength, and pray that we would acquire some common sense. Particularly Lucile's mother, a born teacher and committed Cartesian. My mother had nothing of the professor about her. She truly had nothing to impart. Perhaps this was why she could never relax, why she always seemed to be preparing for the next activity. Before a swim, with her route already marked out, there was nothing to decide. But afterwards? Afterwards she didn't know what to do with her energy. She would fidget, compose shopping lists, go home, go out again, visit her mother, sit with her in the garden and knit, almost immediately feeling the urge to throw the knitting aside and leave. Meanwhile Lucile's mother – was this thanks to Descartes? – was very good at relaxing. She read lying on her front on the sand, glasses perched on the end of her nose. When she got up and moved a little closer to us to try and see what we were up to, she would peer at us vaguely over the top of the novel through whose pages her imagination was wandering.

In spite of their profound differences, they did agree to sign the two of us up to a swimming club. This ought not to have pleased us at all, but we were too bound up with each other to be thrown by the idea of a group activity, and besides we rather liked Monsieur Trimalco, the swimming and gymnastics teacher. He had a lovely voice, plenty of patience and a kind smile, but most of all – and this was the important thing – he was very short and slightly hunchbacked. His handicap was a sign that he was one of us. We saw it as an indication of mental dissidence, a secret identity. Trimalco was not of the race of athletes like the coaches from the two (rival) gymnastics clubs in the town: For the Fatherland and Children of Arcachon. He belonged, like us, to a world of unnameable creatures, charming monsters. When he was teaching us how to dive, he was always the first to throw himself off the stern of the boat; all the children, including us, followed suit. There was no need for Lucile to whisper to me that Trimalco was one of the henchmen of the Princess of the Palace of the Sea, one of her most trusted aides; it was obvious. Under his tutelage, we adored diving. Nothing about it scared us. Neither the fall into emptiness, nor the shock as we met the water. We learnt to high dive, the water catching us on the vertical, submerging us in its depths. We gave in to it, plunging deep, deeper still, then freeing ourselves with a thrust of the pelvis, and climbing back up to the surface, ears ringing. We opened our eyes, bathed in saline tears, and gambolled in a flurry of spray, waves and laughter.

The horizontal bar held marvels. I loved to push myself forward, head down, knees gripping the trapeze, or balance on a giant ball, or take flight on the trampoline – spurred on by the anticipation of bouncing even higher each time I fell. Happiness insinuated itself into the muscles and tendons of my calves, asserted itself in my thighs, carried my entire being in a jubilation of weightlessness. It was like swimming in air.

I loved the net of cords that surrounded the apparatus in the gym, and the floating dinghy of the diving board. They traced new perimeters of experimentation, gave a new framework for our theatre. I learnt to do cartwheels, backbends, the splits. My body was changing.

Gymnastics with Trimalco was entirely unrelated to the laws of symmetry or numbers. He employed none of the tricks and techniques used by grown-ups to entice children into a programme of education in order then to trap them in it. He had more than one trick up his sleeve to foil the syllabus. We considered him an ally in our defence of thwarting norms. A struggle that was, by definition, clandestine.

When it rained the club abandoned the beach, moving into town and sheltering in the local gymnasium. That was out of the question for us. From the smell of sweat in the cloakroom, to the grey lino, knotted climbing ropes and pommel horses screwed to the floor, we wanted none of it. On days when it rained, we walked in the rain. We roamed the streets of Arcachon. We made discoveries – not only streets, alleyways, narrow passages and cul-de-sacs that we never went down on our everyday itineraries, when we always took the main arteries like Avenue Nelly-Deganne and Rue Lamarque-de-Plaisance (which sounded to me like the *mark of pleasants)*, but also the infinite diversity of the rain. Squally, torrential rain that unfurled like a thick curtain and erased the world; deliciously moistening drizzle; punitive rain, that fell diagonally in a regular rhythm, nothing spectacular but capable of lasting a long time. The rain of sad love affairs that didn't make you want to rip off your dress and run naked onto the jetty but simply left you with a sense of nothingness.

All the same we were interested in it, because we sensed in it the intimate tenderness of summer rain and its affinity with the water we swam in – water that seeks nothing more than to wrap you in its embrace.

Our wanderings were not an expression of any kind of hostility to Trimalco. It was simply that we preferred the rain to being shut up inside the gymnasium.

In the same way, when we were summoned by our mothers, we always chose swimming over dinner. To start with. As long as we could.

People had only a secondary role. It was the elements that dictated our behaviour. Sun, rain, wind, sand, tides.

MODESTY

Not only did the club teach me to how to dislocate my joints, clasp my toes, walk like a crab and do the splits, it also taught me modesty. Or at least a certain belief in modesty. I began getting changed with my legs tangled in my towel, and, in consideration of my supposed femininity, I started wearing a bikini top. It didn't fit properly, and one day I lost it when I jumped off the boat. I found myself seized by an incredible, dogged urge to retrieve it. I dived down as deep as I could to try and fish out the two white triangles and the narrow multi-coloured ribbons that tied them on. I held my breath until my lungs were about to burst. But I couldn't find it. Lucile joked: "It's fallen all the way down to the Princess of the Palace of the Sea. You should be happy. It's an honour." I didn't smile. I felt horribly naked, and that triggered a shame whose burning wasn't entirely disagreeable. Lucile teased me endlessly, wondering aloud which of the princess's courtiers was going to wear my bikini top. Her teasing infuriated me. I acted as though I was fine with my skinny torso exposed to the breeze. But secretly I wondered why I was so desperate to retrieve my top when I denied with my entire soul the possibility that my breasts were ever going to develop.

OUT OF MY DEPTH

Some of the boys at the club could walk right into the sea on their hands. They would balance on their arms and wade into the water for as long as they could hold their breath. Sometimes I turned cartwheels into the water. Trimalco taught me a lot. Now I could really swim. According to objective criteria. I went well beyond the stage of flailing about doing doggy-paddle. I could only do a few metres of crawl, no more. My breaststroke, though, was perfect. It would take me wherever I wanted to go, even, I could tell, long distances in unfamiliar seas. But I wasn't interested in swimming a long way down the coast. Doing lengths didn't interest me. My pleasure in my newfound self-confidence manifested itself in the transition (no longer a transition) between when I could still touch the bottom with my feet – when I could stop swimming and still stand – and when I could no longer touch the bottom. It is in that indifference, that feeling of equal serenity whether floating above a metre of water or above the ocean depths, that the true freedom of the swimmer is located. The ability to revel fully in another way of being; the sense of abandon, of letting go. I learnt to go out of my depth. Jubilation, swimming style.

This morning – was it because yesterday evening I wrote "jubilation, swimming style", groping for the right words to describe the sheer euphoria of swimming? – my swim was pure joy. I felt it from my first contact with the water, as I climbed down the little metal ladder fixed to the rocks and stopped for a moment, just long enough to embrace the horizon, the pale, weightless, almost translucent blue of the sky, the blue-green of the sea, tinged with turquoise, a denser blue through which nothing intangible could pass other than – as the sun began to appear from behind the houses and the parasol pines on the hill that dominates the landscape – occasional pools of light expanding into the heart of pure colour. A deep blue intensified by the same penetrating brilliance that irradiates Picasso's paintings. Just a moment to take in the splendour into which I was about to immerse myself. It was with this unfading image before my eyes, this carnival of blue, that I began to swim. The water, barely cooled by last night's rain, was perfect. Its balmy temperature made each stroke more deliciously enveloping than the last, each drawing the next one on, and so on. It's never enough. It came back to me – though without the exuberance of the child and her desire to communicate her revelation to the whole beach (actually no more than four or five people scattered on the rocks) – how swimming summons swimming. I felt that mounting desire that beckons the swimmer to keep going forever. I swam, beginning with breaststroke with my head out of the water, then underwater, then the diagonal art of sidestroke, the pleasure of cleaving the water at an angle.

THE RESIN TAPPER'S HUT

Happiness comes from the sea. It dances in the movement of the waves, is renewed in their constant motion. Even those who don't know how to swim, even people who have come to the seaside just for the day to paddle in the shallows with their trousers rolled or their skirts hitched up, are delighted by it. They hold on to each other, stumble, are sprayed by a wave, shriek with delight. They close their fingers on the water, it trickles away and vanishes. Water can't be controlled. And nor can we: when we go into the water we are no longer completely in control.

We jump and dive, frolic and roll about in the laughing spray.

The forest was a different story. It never made you feel like laughing. I was frightened there. I tended to go there only in autumn and winter. I preferred to go there for a specific purpose, like picking blackberries or foraging for mushrooms. Though in summer too, sometimes, on grey afternoons, we would go to the forest instead of the beach. I liked going with Lucile. She was quite happy in the forest and her composure calmed my fears. The forest became hospitable, no longer a place of gloom and shadow, a black forest. The soaring pines didn't blanket the light. We walked in bright sunlight, our footsteps making no sound on the thick, slightly springy carpet of pine needles.

Having conquered my forebodings I began to enjoy going to the forest. One day we were wandering, randomly, picking heather, comparing ferns, sniffing moss, when we came upon a little wooden hut. It stood in the middle of a clearing torn up by moles. The door had been ripped off and flung into a tangle of nettles. The absence of a door was like an invitation to enter. Instead of panes of glass, half-rotten wooden planks were nailed over the windows, through which a little light crept in. In a corner, dimly visible, chained to each other by spider webs, were a few pieces of broken furniture. The smell of damp cinders and ancient misery pricked our eyes. We should have left but sheer terror pinned us to the spot.

"There's someone here," I said. "They've made a fire."

"No, don't be ridiculous."

"Yes, there is. We should go."

Yet I made no move to leave. We both stood frozen to the spot in the middle of the room.

"Whoever lived here is dead," Lucile whispered, sounding uncertain. Just then we heard something clatter to the floor in the cobwebby corner. I saw a little man, his eyes glowing in the shadows. Lucile grabbed my hand and pulled me to the doorway. We ran through the nettles and the gorse, legs burning, hearts beating furiously. We were so panicked that we completely forgot our rule never to tell our parents anything.

We shouted that we had seen a man in a hut, a man with an axe in his hand. He was going to kill us. I said: "He had eyes like a fox." My grandmother tried to reassure us. There was no one there. The hut had been abandoned years before by the resin tapper who lived there with his family. "Yes, it's a resin tapper's hut," agreed my mother. "What were you doing playing there? It's creepy. Not dangerous, but depressing. I hate those huts," she said. The vehemence of this avowal was exactly the same as when she declared, "I absolutely loathe the kind of person who resigns themselves to a situation. I prefer a good dose of anger. You explode and then two minutes later everything's forgotten." With these words she was taking a potshot at my father's silence, his tendency to avoid explanation and conflict. But what did that have to do with what we had just witnessed? None whatsoever, except that I had mixed up *resin* and *resigned*. On reflection it seemed strange to me that someone who was resigned, passive, prepared to accept anything as long as he was left alone, a taciturn person who simply kept to himself, would want to murder us just because we had entered his house without an invitation.

"It doesn't make sense," I said to Lucile, as we were walking home. "I don't think there was really anybody there." Lucile wasn't listening. She was talking to my mother. She asked her, "Do you like the oyster shacks?" We loved them but Lucile didn't tell her that. Once our panic had dissipated we recovered our instinct for secrecy. Our plan was one day to live in an oyster shack. We were each going to choose one. I still couldn't decide on the colour, but I never tired of imagining its oyster shell garden, the dazzling whiteness.

SEE YOU NEXT SUMMER!

We were completely unaware of the days passing. Then one September evening, the beach long since emptied of vacationing children whose departure we had barely noticed, our mothers exchanged a few pleasantries, finishing up with, "Say goodbye, you two; see you next summer!"

The great dune toppled on top of us, the jetties collapsed, the bay emptied, the crabs scuttled off, the jellyfish were transfixed, the oysters sang at the tops of their voices, the seagulls fell silent – and our mothers turned into nagging harridans. "Come on," they chivvied, as if nothing was wrong. "Hurry up, it's time to go." We hugged each other briefly. In dull voices we repeated, "Bye, see you next summer," and then we walked away, each in the direction decreed by our mother. We didn't turn around. It might have been sunny or overcast; it made no difference any more. At the exact moment that the end of the season had been ordained, the magical bond that linked us to the elements was broken. We no longer obeyed the wind, or swam with the current; we heard no more news of the princess.

HOMONYMS

At home, at the beach, in shops, the word *mama* fluttered endlessly in the air. It wasn't me who uttered it, but my mother, addressing her mother – calling her, asking her advice, talking about her, arguing with her (though never seriously, more like a child trying to disobey). My family space was steeped in the word *mama*, as it had been since long before I was born. I tried not to say it myself. I didn't understand how this word could be used to refer to a unique, irreplaceable being, a child in frantic desperation calling for its mother.

One day I was at the Eyrac beach, building a labyrinthine fortress with some other children, my year-round playmates (I'd had no problem being let back into the group). Everyone was busy. The tide was coming in: the inland pools were gradually being swallowed up by the sea, soon our edifice would be a peninsula, then an island, then... No one could bear to imagine what would happen after that. "Chantal!" I stood up. "My mother's calling me, I'll be back in a minute." She overheard what I said and, sounding hurt, asked me: "Why did you say 'my mother' and not 'mama'?" We were standing with our feet in the shallows. She had her bathing cap in her hand and was shaking her head to give some volume to her brown, wavy, shoulder-length hair. As I stood looking up at her, the way she shook her head made this manifestation of her displeasure seem even more severe. I didn't answer. I contemplated responding, "I thought it meant the same thing," but the recognition of my bad faith held me back. *Mama* is more affectionate, more naturally and ardently possessive than *mother*. *Mama* chimes, both for and within everyone, with a unique resonance. I had an inkling of it, but because the music of this exclusivity escaped me, I preferred to avoid it.

We took a few steps together without speaking. I concentrated on the sound of our feet splashing in the shallows. My mother, always swift to change the subject of conversation (even when it was pleasant), sent me back to the sand fortress. "Careful not to catch a chill in your wet costume!"

One day, in a French lesson, the teacher was explaining to us the difference between a homonym and a synonym. We had to write down some examples. For my homonyms I wrote *mère* and *mer* – *mother* and *sea*; *foi* and *foie* – *faith* and *liver*. I also thought of *résigné* and *résinier*, *resigned* and *resin tapper*, *resigned* and *resin*, but I kept that one for myself. I couldn't think of any synonyms. I didn't believe that two different words could really mean the same thing.

DICTATION

After we did a dictation in school, we all had to sit and correct it together in class. I could never bear to admit that there was only one way to spell a word. It infuriated me when my attempts that didn't agree *exactly* with the officially sanctioned versions were accused of being errors. I hated the way that errors, like confession, were calibrated according to a strict hierarchy: just as there are venal sins and mortal sins, so it is with spelling errors. It was not too terrible to damage a noun; it was extremely serious to make a mistake in a verb. If I wrote *daffoddil, dafodil, dafoddil,* I lost one mark. If I allowed myself *goinng* – because I was so very happy to be going that I wanted to draw out the consonants – I paid a high price.

Why didn't I have a choice? Who was it who had decreed for all eternity the correct way for a word to be spelled? God? His deputy in charge of Scriptures? The official in charge of exercise books? Why was a formal decision taken to put an end to the metamorphosis of words? In the absence of Lucile, I asked my grandfather. I knew that Lucile was very good at dictation.

This was logical, given that she had a mother whose head was always in a book and who taught literature. Her mother even talked like a dictation. Unusual words in long, perfectly modulated sentences. This was not entirely reassuring. Listening to her I could never stop myself wondering which famous author was speaking through her. When my mother spoke I was certain it came from her; no writer, however extraordinary, ever expressed herself through my mother's mouth. It was *her*. My mother was not a medium for anyone.

It was very windy. Félix and I sat perched on the seawall. He was wearing a beret pulled tight over his head and a beige raincoat. I had on my red anorak, a grey pleated skirt and light blue ankle socks. I was always delighted to go for a walk with my grandfather. I would have been in a wonderful mood if it had not been for my post-dictation queasiness, the feeling of persecution, or, more objectively, institutional injustice.

The sea was moving in tight, pointy waves, like *accents circonflexes*, as our teacher would have said (perhaps). The beach was empty. The only marks on the sand were the faint imprints of bird feet. Fishing smacks heading out towards the oyster beds sailed by the jetty. The sound of their motors accompanied our words and our silences with the regular rhythm of a beating heart.

"God has nothing to do with it," Félix assured me. "When it comes to writing, God is only interested in the Holy Scriptures. Not little girls doing dictations."

"So whose fault is it then?"

"Nobody's. Usage."

"What's usage?"

Usage, *sewage*, the words sounded the same to me. I imagined threadbare words, slumped, lethargic; verbal rags incapable of reinventing themselves or of taking pleasure at the idea of surprising us every time we met. Not necessarily big differences, just a light touch, thanks to which no moment would ever be exactly the same, so that it would be essential to really savour it: one letter more or less, an extra accent, the sound of the letter *h* occasionally suppressed.

I imagined... Did I really have to imagine it? Was I not witness everywhere, day after day, to words chosen precisely because they had been overused, for their guaranteed banality? Were my ears not already saturated with exchanges whose tacit agreement was that nothing whatsoever was to be expressed of the despair that was consuming you, the love that had vanished, the silence that was gradually engulfing all the rooms in the dwelling of your soul? My grandfather had a different way of speaking. He believed in living speech. He *was* living speech. And a truly open mind: he saw in the architecture of the clouds as much presence as in that created by humans.

I was struggling at school, and not only with dictation. In fact I thought that all schoolwork could be called dictation, because school is a place where there is always someone to dictate what you can and cannot do. Even the time when you are supposed to play is dictated. School doesn't conceal its predilection for multiplication tables, rules of grammar, conjugation charts, lists of all the French départements. School abhors those who worship the Mud Sprite. School is a vast organization on the model of the Lesson family. My mother regarded this organization with the same hostility she bore towards all notions of groups and classification. My mother did not like school. She encouraged me to play truant. Without my even asking she would offer to write me a note saying that I was ill. But as far as I was concerned not liking school was not a reason not to attend. I was extremely assiduous. Everything that school refused to acknowledge about the sovereignty of metamorphosis (in other words all that was fundamental to the life of and on the bay), everything based on the belief in a fixed universe, disturbed me. I sensed a serious challenge that couldn't be dismissed with a flick of the finger, something to be explored in depth; perhaps there was even the possibility of discovering a parallel universe. I also refused to allow illness to have any place in my life, even if only to serve as a pretext or a lie, because I had obscurely guessed from the drastic changes in my mother that an illness did not have to be "real" in order to destroy.

THE TOWN, WINTER

When you reach a holiday destination, particularly a seaside resort, you put into parentheses not only everything that has taken place in your life before you got there, but also everything that preceded you in the place you've just arrived at. Where, if not on the sand, will the history of a beach be written? Where, if not in a song, is the expression of summer? Perhaps that means that neither the beach nor summertime, nor their part-time bit players – vacationing tourists – have a history. When people like my parents decide to settle down permanently in a seaside resort, it's surely because they are seeking refuge in a place of emptiness or nothingness. Doing so implies that they know how to live off nothing, or almost nothing: how to find excitement in the tiniest detail, delight in minuscule shades of difference, become expert at modelling the tides and the fluctuating route of the waves, or the alchemy of the blue, or the flight of the grey heron. It assumes the ability to hold on to the carefree holiday spirit as days and seasons roll by, the capacity to delight in the present moment. It is to take a risk that echoes the child's hope for her whole life: that she will manage to experience afresh every morning the unspoilt beauty of Arcachon Bay. But if they fail to hold on to that carefree feeling, if the blessing of that first morning is allowed to slip away, then monotony takes over and their mood risks sliding into neurasthenia, where life unfurls before a magnificent landscape, but its beauty is touristic, a backdrop balanced precariously on the edge of a void. My father had locked himself up inside a citadel of silence. My mother was drifting, in constant fear of illness. She was a little more animated during the summer, but less and less cheerful. Her dark compass was oriented towards the winter. With her housewife's boredom and the depression that went with it, she preferred the primarily medical character of Arcachon's most famous neighbourhood, Winter Town. That was where she went to see her doctors, with whom she was endlessly disappointed. Sometimes I went with her. We would push open the gate and go through the front door of one or other of these old villas, or "chalets", built in the middle of the 19th century, when people used to come to Arcachon to be treated for tuberculosis. It was as though the history of the town – in which she had no interest, indeed whose reality she denied – was catching up with her like a curse. In her exclusive adoption of Summer Town, her passion for holidays and complete lack of interest in her own recent suffering in Winter Town, the neighbourhood of fever and death, she was unknowingly reproducing the political decision that had seen the medical character of the town erased in order to promote the seaside resort, which was built upon the elimination of every disturbing trace of illness. A seaside resort is switched off at the end of the season. It is not switched on again until the following summer, with the arrival of the first visitors of the season.

We would leave the doctor's office, my mother carrying her new prescription and I the novel I had brought to read in the waiting room, breathing in air redolent with the perfumed foliage. We walked through Winter Town's crescents, neither of us aware that the streets had been designed like that to protect patients convalescing in this verdant sanctuary from stormy weather blowing in from the sea.

Curiously, I got a nurse's uniform for Christmas that year, a white blouse and cap, embroidered with a red cross (in cross stitch), and a nurse's bag. I dressed up in it sometimes to make the child next door suffer (poultice of pine resin, tincture of iodine water), but I wasn't particularly excited about it. I was quite capable of making her suffer without needing to get decked out in a white hat and blouse.

The following Christmas I was given a pair of stilts which I absolutely adored. I strode through the streets. Passers-by, hearing the hammering of wooden-soled limbs, thought that a disabled person was walking behind them. As they were about to move thoughtfully aside they would turn around and their surprise at seeing a little girl towering over them made me laugh – a little girl on stilts, like the three houses on the Isle of Birds… I was tall and fast; but that didn't mean I wouldn't also be small and slow, smaller than nature, tomorrow, soon, in the springtime, when I would go back to swimming in the sea, to being tossed on the waves, and continuing my important study of the minuscule life of seashells, tracing with the tip of my tongue their pearly concavities, their torqued beauty and fan-like openings, slipping right inside the periwinkle's black spiral to really fathom it.

BATHED IN SWEAT

I must have seemed fragile, or else it was my mother projecting her anxieties onto me. In any case, she couldn't stop herself, as soon as the weather began to cool down, from layering me with mittens, scarf, hat, hood, cagoule and a sweater. In winter she made me put on a first layer against my skin, a vile woollen vest knitted by my aunt Élodie. It itched. It was monstrous. (The inspiration for my aunt Élodie's woollen creations must have been the original hair shirt.) At the small private school I went to, the rules forbade the wearing of trousers. The uniform was a navy blue jacket and pleated skirt, no trousers, no troubling games between the sexes (for the same reason we were forbidden to play cops and robbers. There was to be no passing from one category of person to another, particularly when one category was criminal). This saddened my mother. She couldn't understand why, when it was so cold, we had to go to school with bare legs – even though she herself was a devotee of bare legs.

The result of all these precautions was that I was often bathed in sweat – a state and an expression that I found repulsive.

Most sports require putting on lots of bulky kit: boots or heavy shoes, tights, trunks, tracksuit, leg-warmers, shoulder braces, body armour, helmets, gloves, kneepads; protecting jaws with screens and eyes with tinted sunglasses and visors; supporting the lower back; attaching ropes, putting on crampons, and so on. For swimming, all you need to do is take off your clothes.

Without being able to explain why, I sensed a connection between the nurse's uniform and my mother's obsession with dressing me too warmly.

THE HAND WAVING AT THE BOTTOM OF THE SEA

It was October. I was in secondary school. My towel was laid out on the sand, alongside it not my beach bag but my satchel, its brown leather battered from serving variously as recipient, projectile and shield. It was sitting on a pile of kelp. From a distance the two looked the same. As if my satchel were made of kelp, or the parcels of knowledge crammed inside my satchel could not resist the marine weed. I had rushed out of school and careered on my bicycle down Avenue Gambetta so that I would be sure to get there in time to swim. The water wasn't warm, but it still had something of the mildness of summer. Both the sea and the beach were empty. It was low tide and the beach was huge. I walked into the water, focused on my sensations; at first the cold made me want to cry out, the nip of those initial moments so intense that it only made the mildness of the water, its incipient warmth, more palpable. Four, five strokes and it was perfect; I succumbed to its balmy embrace. I swam straight ahead, confident, towards the grey-blue horizon. I swam sufficiently far out that I could no longer touch the bottom. I was floating, completely relaxed. And then, for no reason (or perhaps to better savour my amazing aptitude for floating), I peered down into the depths, only to see a long, pale hand, its wrist joint caught in the sand, its fingers waving gently. I swam as fast as I could back to the shore, with the waving hand at the bottom of the sea in pursuit, trying to grab me. I opened my mouth but no sound came out.

Back on dry land, my heart beating wildly, I lay down on the sand and was overwhelmed by a fear so violent, a panic so perfect, that I felt an extraordinary rush of well-being, a pleasure superior even to that which, instinctively and in complete innocence, I had learnt to give myself a long time ago. Legs wobbly, hair dripping, feeling the coolness of the sand through the absorbent fabric of my towel, I understood then that you never completely master going out of your depth.

This made me extraordinarily happy.

The following summer was the year I began to go dancing at the Mauresque casino. I encountered the city by night. Boys' breath, their lips on my skin. After the dance we would hang around the park, weaving in and out of its paths, its ghosts and grottos, its palm trees and rose bushes. Sometimes, as if hypnotized, we would be drawn back to the huge, brightly lit room with its marble columns, arabesques and carved gothic arches, flashes of gold reflected in the huge mirrors. Afterwards we would go down to the beach and make love. The water was blacker than the blackest of shadows, all its light buried in the pale sand and the flashes of nudity exposed by our frenzied hands. Every night I journeyed to the Orient. Every night, I ventured a little deeper into the feverish maze.

Heeding my religious conscience, with the approach of Assumption Day on 15th August and the festival of the blessing of the boats, I went to confess my "impure acts". The priest urged me to be more explicit and then proceeded to scold me with the example of the Virgin Mary. He gave me twenty Hail Marys. I knelt and transformed myself into a prayer mill: *Hail Mary full of grace the Lord is with thee blessed art thou among women and blessed is the fruit of thy womb Jesus.* Heat rose in me at the memory of certain acts. I stood up, made the sign of the cross, walked back down the nave and smiled at the sun outside. A voice whispered to me: *It doesn't matter whose hands those fingers pleasuring you belong to: you, some man, the sea.*

NATHANAËL, I WILL TEACH YOU PASSION

My mother was already up. She prepared her bag with the same swift, spritely movements as always. Depression never produced the slightest hint of sluggishness in her. She said goodbye to me – she always said *ciao* for *au revoir* and *hello* for *bonjour*. In spite of being depressed, she never interiorized her depression. Being unhappy did not fit her vision of the world. Fundamentally she did not buy into the notion of sadness, either in herself or in others, which was why anger won out over all other emotions. I watched her leave. She walked on the damp sand exactly as she did on dry sand, her steps leaving no imprint. I wondered what she was daydreaming about, as she sat on her little towel on the beach, her eyes turned towards the sea. About the career as a sporting star she had once believed was her destiny? For years she replayed, over and over again, the brief silent film of her youthful dream. Eventually it lost its sharpness, until all she could remember of the swimming trial that established her as a champion was the churning foam. In truth, she didn't recognize herself in the image of the swimmer who was the first to reach the end, cheered on by the crowd. She only knew from her father's triumphant smile as he stood and clapped that the victory was hers. Over time the scene remained unchanged, just as her life now was on a loop, though stripped of the slightest chance of applause. Is there anything in the daily life of a housewife, in the constantly resuming sequence of her activities, which could ever provoke such enthusiasm? Who, seeing a housewife making a bed or scrubbing a pot, is going to jump up and down with excitement, shouting *encore*? Alas – and this ironic cruelty was at the heart of it – every housewife knows that tomorrow she will have to do it all over again, with no spectator cheering her on; such is the silent lot of her toil. Repetition is her fate, never with any hope of an ovation.

I doubt Jackie was still replaying the film in her mind's eye. She had given up on dreaming. Looking at the sky, she would try to predict the weather and the options and conditions for tomorrow's swim. She had returned to the real world, her real life, its shallow wake as swiftly erased as that of her swimmer's body imprinted on the water.

"I never have anything new to look forward to," she would complain. I didn't know how to convince her otherwise. Somehow I understood that newness doesn't spontaneously come from outside oneself. It's something you yourself have to put there, in order for it to manifest itself and break the visible monotony – a sensitivity to detail, a predilection for nuance, a passion for the moment. Days by the sea follow on from one another like a suite of variations that can be so subtle that an observer from elsewhere, whether a traveller passing through or someone locked inside their own unhappiness, would never notice its nuances. Yet nothing is ever exactly the same, whether the interval between the tides, the colour of the water, the shape of the clouds – or the shiver that goes through me when I dive. The range of those shivers, I tell myself in a moment of lyricism, is as intricate and open to unexpected developments as a sunrise.

All winter, my mother rushed from one doctor to another. At each visit, she was prescribed different medicines, injections, pills, tablets, syrups and disgusting potions. None would admit that this woman, who had no reason to be so, was unhappy. Some – perhaps thinking of their own wives – were angry with her for finding ordinary life unbearable. One of them, whether through unconscious resentment or naive faith in the efficiency of the latest fashionable treatment, recommended that she saw a psychiatrist in Bordeaux, who in turn sent her to a clinic for electroshock therapy, in which electrodes were attached to the patient's skull to deliver a current. Epilepsy as a remedy for depression. She was so desperate that she underwent the electric shocks. When she came back she was listless, her eyes dead.

She grew thin, her beauty faded. It was as if another woman had taken her place. And that spring, under a clear sky, while there was still a nip in the air, when it was time to test the waters – starting with the toes, going in up to the calves, then all the way to the critical, ultra-sensitive area at the top of the thighs – she declared that she was too thin to be seen undressed, and that she would swim later on in the evening, when there was no one around to stare.

Meanwhile I had begun swimming earlier and earlier in the day. The sea had cooled down in the night air. The beach was empty. The comings and goings of human beings had not yet scrambled the delicate imprints of the seabirds' feet. I always took care not to rub them away as I walked towards the sea. This morning swim in the sheer blue, the silence broken only by a passing fishing smack, filled me with the thrill of an exercise in determination. I felt as though my steadfast and resolute forward progress was the physical proof of an innate willingness to confront challenges, overcome obstacles and achieve whatever I desired. I was reading André Gide's *The Fruits of the Earth*. Gide thrilled me: I copied out his sentences in a notebook and learnt them by heart. I repeated to myself:

It is not enough for me to read that the sand on the beach is soft, I want my feet to feel it.

All knowledge that is not preceded by sensation is pointless.

Never seek, Nathanaël, to taste the waters of the past again.

Nathanaël, throw away my book; tell yourself that it is only one of the thousand possible postures facing you in life. Find your own...

Nathanaël. Nathaniel. In my giddy excitement I thought that Gide was addressing the man who had given his name to my street, and that according to some mystical relationship of proximity I was included in his message. Inspired, I emerged from the water with the feeling that I possessed incredible reserves of strength, a deep well to be drawn from only for occasional, irrevocable decisions.

These swims were quite different from my usual style. I liked to float, to swim in order to dissolve myself, to become one with the water as it streamed through my fingers like softly flowing sand. By nature and by choice I liked to let myself drift on the current, be carried by the tide. Languid, aimless swims ought to have been enough for me. I had no reason to be up so early, my head buzzing with aphorisms. I had no reason to swap my usual leisurely dips for energetic swimming. But, actually, yes, I did have a reason, or at least an intuition. Something told me that being a wanderer, retaining an openness to the world, cannot be taken for granted: maintaining it requires vigilance, entails a certain discipline.

THE LAST SUMMER

One day, very unusually, my mother came down to the beach in the afternoon. And – even more unusually – she was with my father. It was high tide, and the beach was no more than a narrow ribbon of sand. The water was deep green and very calm. They sat down side by side. I was lying farther down the beach, drying off in the sun. They hadn't seen me. I got up to move closer to them. I caught my mother's words: "I can't go on any more." I moved farther up the beach away from them. I couldn't bear to hear her despair. Like the doctors who thought she was a hypochondriac, a hysterical, spoilt little girl, I had no sympathy for her suffering. I didn't want to admit any more than they did that ordinary life could push you to extremes – I didn't want to admit it was true *for her*, even if I promised myself that I would never fall into that trap. I waved at them then raced off to hang around the jetty. The jetty still seemed as immense as it had when I was little. It looked as though it projected far out to sea. Going off to explore the jetty was a way of putting a distance between us, not quite as far as on a boat, but almost. I don't know what my father answered, or if he said anything at all: since he didn't have the words to express his own sadness, how was he going to find the words to comfort her? When I turned around I saw them going into the water together.

It was our last summer in Arcachon. My father's last summer. He died on 2nd January the following year. A premature death: he was only forty-three, though it was, according to the incomprehensible death certificate issued by the clinic, physiologically explicable. There was nothing to add, no reason to contest it. It was sad, but that's life. And life includes death, it would be crazy to say otherwise. Which means I must have been crazy, because I truly believed that life, real life, wants nothing to do with death, in any way, in any disguise. Death is the absolute enemy of life. The Sand and Sea were, no doubt, made to be reconciled, but not Life and Death. Between them there is no plausible arrangement, not even the spindliest bridge. Once you go down the alley with no name, once you cross the dark river, there is no possibility of return... As far as I was concerned there was every reason to rise up and broadcast this grievance across the entire ocean, to howl into the empty expanse of the sky that there is no such thing as a "natural" death. I believed it, I was convinced – but my young, dead father had bequeathed me the legacy of silence. Out of that muted, dull matter, out of that premature grave, I was going to have to extract my own words, from which I would effect, by some assemblage of homonyms and synonyms, the slow, gradual unearthing of my own language. In those sandy ruins, in the very impossibility of speech, I was going to have to try and find my strength.

II
OTHER SHORES

DREAM

My mother, young, around forty. The age she was when she arrived on the Côte d'Azur. At first she is a silhouette on a postcard, then, with no transition, a real person standing in front of a window in my room in Paris. I am afraid to take her in my arms.

MOVING HOUSE

Unexpectedly now a widow, Jackie returned to work as a shorthand typist (though this time without any gymnastic exploits), but she was mainly focused on preparing her departure from Arcachon. Displaying a hitherto entirely unsuspected faculty for decisiveness and organization, she took responsibility for every aspect of the operation. She put the house on Avenue George-VI, which they had only recently moved into, on the market. She set about getting rid of suitcases filled with old papers, either on a bonfire, or by calling junk merchants, or simply by throwing them in the bin: out of date documents and photos, plus old clothes, and a lot of ornaments and small items of furniture. She threw away trunks dating from the era when luggage could not be carried (even when empty they weighed a ton). She got rid not only of all the things she didn't care about, but also of everything that was, as she put it, "too upsetting", including Félix's war diaries and the many watercolours he had painted – the seashore in all its different lights, flocks of seagulls in flight, all the shades of the yellow sand, dreamy paintings of cabins on stilts, pine cones, festoons of gorse, the low skies he recalled from his childhood in Brittany, chapels and shrines... Big Doll didn't escape the upheaval either. Her brooches and white leather lace-up shoes, the knots in her hair! Often when I am travelling, with my penchant for flea markets and particularly for displays of toys and abandoned dolls, especially the really pathetic ones – the ones with an eye that won't open, a broken wrist, a hairpiece half unstuck – I daydream that Big Doll, the forebear of all my dolls, my mother's, my grandmother Eugénie's, my great-grandmother Zélie's, the doll who had tried so hard to teach me to see beyond the marvels of the present, the unimaginable passage of years and centuries, Time Doll, will be lying there among her companions in neglect, laid out like them on top of a tatty blanket, the lid of a packing case, a sheet of newspaper, or simply on the ground, at the risk of being stepped on, so damaged, dirty, disfigured and broken that I don't recognize her. Sometimes I retrace my steps to peer closely, against all visible evidence, at the rag doll with yellow wool hair and two red dots on her cheeks, the violinist wearing a pair of "proper little girl" trousers, the skinny, ebony-black doll with hair tightly braided in cornrows balancing on the edge of the pavement, or the Amazonian doll fashioned out of twisted wire, following intently from beneath lowered eyelids the power of her hold on a wistful little girl. I sense their eyes on me, their trembling presence, their desire to come alive again. In their damaged fortunes, the glimmers of their miraculously preserved beauty, I see fragments of their incomplete histories, the childhoods they were driven away from and to which they would happily return at any moment, with their poised compliance and admirable ability to remain indifferent to this period of indigence and destitution.

Jackie was not blessed with the resistant carapace of these maltreated dolls. Now she was on the point of leaving, she was discarding and forgetting as much as she could. She was entirely devoid of affection for what she was leaving behind, and yet she was filled with regret: simultaneously determined and desolate. In the same way that it often seems that the more miserable their lives the more afraid people are to die, she wept to be leaving the town she had lived in as a married woman. She wept for her wasted love, thinking, in her suffering and sadness, of the curse that keeps tightly bound to one another, if only by incomprehension, those couples who are as incapable of happiness together as of separating. As if this incomprehension were a kind of cement between people. An opaque substance, caught within which they are each fighting their own corner. In this unhappiness, as wearying as it is pointless, a man will tend to mire himself in silence, while a woman is more likely to lose her head in nonsense, chattering about anything and everything, aware that she is infuriating her partner, the Superior Silent

One, provoking his contempt each time a little more, and, in the same calamitous movement, widening the chasm that both separates them and binds them to one another. My mother wept as she planned her departure from Arcachon. She was both awash in self-pity and highly organized. She took as little with her as possible, but it was still a big move. Her heart wavered between unfocused sorrow and genuine relief (however unavowed) as she sealed up boxes and kept an eye on the removal men.

She was, however, decisive when it came to choosing her destination. She was fleeing the Côte d'Argent for the Côte d'Azur, swapping Cap Ferret for Cap Ferrat, leaving Arcachon for Menton. One coastal resort for another, both sheltered enclaves. In her quest for boundless holiday time, she was sure that she had found somewhere far superior. In this sense, she shared the conviction that Flaubert ascribes to Emma Bovary – the unsurpassed heroine of conjugal boredom and chronic indecision, of sentimental narcissism and imagined romantic love. Like her, Jackie believed that happiness is like a plant that flourishes in some soils and withers in others. In the sands of Arcachon, a terrain where almost nothing takes root, her cultivation had not been a success. She needed to find a more fertile soil. She needed to find the right region, or more precisely the right shore. She used to be sure that it was easier to find happiness when one lived near the sea. Now she knew that wasn't enough, although it remained an indispensable element.

Strangely, with the decision to turn her back on Arcachon, she was repeating, after an interval of four centuries, the same trajectory as that of the town's founder (so dear to my grandfather) Brother Thomas, the tormented hermit, who, after the miraculous rescue of Mary and her child, had succumbed to even greater mental distress, and eventually decided to leave Arcachon. Like Jackie, he left the Côte d'Argent for the Côte d'Azur, Arcachon Bay for the Bay of Menton; he exchanged isolation in the company of just a handful of sailors and shepherds who barely spoke Gascon for Monaco and its court, where once again he was able, this time in Italian, to inveigh against the vices of the wealthy and the abuses of the powerful. Like him, though without invoking the Word of God, she was guided by her instinct for life.

Jackie got rid of everything that was "too upsetting" (without daring to say it out loud, she was an adept of the nihilism that holds that a person's death should be followed by the destruction of all their personal effects), keeping only what reminded her of happy, carefree times. She packed a garnet leather-covered photo album in her suitcase, rather than sending it on with the movers. (In the same spirit, she didn't hold on to a single one of my school reports, but she did keep my notebook of song lyrics, a little yellow spiral-bound pad with my name, *Chantal*, written on the cover – the word *chant* tucked inside – and *Arcachon, Gironde* underneath, which I must have thought was enough of my address.) On the first page of the photo album, inscribed in white on the dark card, beneath the cut-out windows for sliding pictures into: *Sport*, *Holidays*, *Joy*, *Sun*. Each word, in Félix's neat, sloping handwriting, had been carefully underlined with a ruler. It was like a kind of schedule inscribed at the beginning of the album. A bright, happy schedule. This wasn't Jackie's anarchic handwriting, her hasty scrawl. Nor would she ever have written on anything so fine. Her handwriting was all over the place, hard for anyone else to decipher, though it barely mattered, since she only jotted things down for herself on scraps of torn paper (which were almost immediately mislaid) – reminders, shopping lists, messages.

Sport, *Holidays*, *Joy*, *Sun*: this was where she picked up the interrupted schedule. Though with plenty of restrictions regarding *Sport*, which for her was no longer simply a question of swimming: thanks to the strange fervour that she put into it, it went well beyond a straightforward sporting commitment, and it made clear how futile, mechanical and interchangeable were all the other sports that she had taken up and then abandoned.

A year earlier, when everything seemed "black" to her, she had suggested that I spend a week in Nice to explore the equation *sun + beauty = joy*. It was August.

After the sandy beaches of the Atlantic I found the beaches of Nice oppressive. To see the sea I had to position myself right by the water, in front of the crowds that were massed behind me, at the very point where the pebbly slope began to tumble into the water. It felt like I was about to fall down too. The lack of space was exacerbated by the ordeal of walking barefoot on the pebbles. Instead of discovering a flash of elation in a higher register, I found an impossible beach with no room to lie down and stretch out, no comfortable place to lounge. The intense blue of the sea looked as though it had been varnished; it was magnificent, but its splendour held me at bay. Its beauty was utterly exteriorized, offering no shelter. It had no low-key register. I was horrified by all the exposed bodies, the unabashed atmosphere of sex. I asked a man where the nearest bank was and he replied, "How much do you want?"

Jackie didn't use this brief trip to make any kind of plan for herself; she wasn't dreaming of her escape (she was completely lacking in malice, and would never have been so nasty as to wish for her husband's death, nor did she have the energy required to imagine moving anywhere with him); nonetheless, retrospectively, it seems obvious that she sent me there as a scout, to bring back some of that Azur light, to roam the streets, sit in the parks and walk on the Promenade des Anglais in her place, to gaze with an enchanted eye on everything that surrounded me.

POSTCARDS

Jackie chose Menton, a small town that was originally in Italy and today is situated next to the border. An oasis in the hollow of a bay, whose old town, dominated by the colours of ochre and saffron, is ranged like an amphitheatre high above the immense blue of the Mediterranean. She emigrated to the furthest point of France, almost to Italy; in some senses it already was Italy, in its music, its colours, its flavours, its art of abundance and overabundance. She had left behind her the silent streets, the mourning black and the monochrome landscapes in which all life's monotony was condensed. She moved to a flat in an apartment complex called Les Aloès. The hill you had to climb to get there was dotted with gardens that overflowed with violet clusters of bougainvillea, hibiscus flowers and acanthus leaves, jasmine and lemon trees heavy with fruit. Eucalyptus, olive and aloe trees grew all over the gardens of her apartment complex.

I, meanwhile, went to live in New York, which I had first visited during a stopover between Lima and Paris. My mother and I communicated by postcard. I sent her pictures of the Empire State Building and the World Trade Centre against a background of the sun setting (I taught French on the sixty-seventh floor of the World Trade Centre, in a special language school for businessmen who had neither the time nor the inclination to study; on postcards of Washington Square I could point towards the East Village – a neighbourhood largely overlooked by photographers – where I imparted the beauties of the French language in overheated apartments belonging to various drunken American and South American poets. In one of those apartments I used to "teach", swinging in a hammock while Astor Piazzolla's tango music played in the background). She sent me views of picturesque narrow streets and baroque facades, the Saint-Antoine gate, the flagstone esplanade in front of the Saint-Michel church, grotesque figures on floats during the citrus festival modelled entirely out of fruit, and the allegorical statue of Music in the casino gardens, from every angle. What luck to have discovered postcards! At last, we had found our means of communication. We wrote to each other in a euphoria of new beginnings and in a tone that had nothing in common with all that had come before – nor, I suspect, very much in common with what either of us was really feeling at that point. It's difficult to imagine a state of mind that could be summed up by a flash of blue sky on a postcard. As Jackie was always in a hurry (I suspect that she scribbled these messages sitting at a table in a café, on her knees, or even in the street, leaning against the letterbox that was about to swallow them up) her writing was virtually illegible. She was so chaotic that it seemed as though her untidiness had actually been enriched and nourished by the almost tropical luxuriance of her new home. Once the address had been written, all she had to do was pour out a warm rain of kisses and the rest of the postcard was filled up. There was barely space for any other words. There was no point in launching into an attempt at describing her days, and even less into introspection. A drop of moisture to stick the stamp, and *voilà*! The link between us could set off on its merry way. The geographical distance was an advantage for her. About once a month I received my lovely shower of kisses from which not a single phrase of any consequence, not one sentence composed of carefully chosen words or considered expressions communicating any genuine sentiment, ever emerged. I began to understand why she liked shorthand typing so much, that technique for transforming sentences into a code that can be rapidly transcribed. That was what she liked about her job as a typist: capturing dictated sentences and reducing them to a few useful signs. Just like when she was a young swimmer racing against herself, she was possessed by the idea of beating her own time. Even her kisses, abbreviated markings condensed out of lengthier formulations, seemed to me a form of shorthand. They were enough for me. In the symmetrical game of our postal communication, they allowed me to remain, like her, at a level of easy exchange, to continue in the register of avoidance, thanks to which the shaky relationship between us remained unsaid, unfixed, able to change.

My mother was the antithesis of that famous letter writer, Madame de Sévigné, which was definitely a good thing, I would tell myself as I extracted her latest postcard from the narrow metal letterbox in the lobby of my apartment building. Who would want to be Françoise-Marguerite, Countess of Grignan, daughter of the Marquise? Such indecent deployment of the maternal possessive! If only that was really what it was all about, rather than being simply the only way for the Marquise to demonstrate her stylistic virtuosity and give free reign to her literary genius, a prerogative otherwise reserved for men... The Marquise did not waste time soul-searching. The confusion between the need to write and the need to write *to her daughter* worked in her favour. Her quill danced over the page. In her enthusiasm for being both mother and writer, two or three times a week she sent her daughter a letter that ranged from ten to thirty pages (my letterbox wouldn't have had room for them). I thought of the addressee, the Countess of Grignan, married to an older man already twice-widowed, probably syphilitic and certainly debt-ridden. He had taken her to live in the Château de Grignan, known as the "Versailles of

Provence". Far from finding this flattering, she was distraught; in cahoots with her mother, she had been hoping to become the mistress of Louis XIV. "The Versailles of bandit country," she would mutter to herself as she closed the windows against the mistral, wishing that the wretched wind would carry her off. But no, it didn't even succeed in blowing away her mother's latest letter. The envelope was still sitting on the secretaire. She hesitated, then decided to open it. "Haymaking is the prettiest thing in the whole world," she read. But of course! And sowing, hoeing, ploughing, killing pigs, how adorable! Or, on her latest pregnancy: "My God, *ma bonne*, how I worry about your belly! And it is not only you whom it is suffocating!" her mother wrote, with unrestrained empathy. The Marquise existed in symbiosis with her daughter's body in its perfection as well as in all the metamorphoses of a woman who would soon be wrecked by a series of pregnancies. She was ready to withdraw without ceremony as soon as Françoise-Marguerite seemed ready in turn to behave like a mother. "Your son went three hours without relieving himself. You were already completely dismayed. Ah! Truly, look at you so amiable with your maternal love: what madness!" This was Françoise-Marguerite being called to order. The degree of her mother's maternal love was not something that could be transmitted. "Please God allow me to love him one day as much as I love you," she wrote.

The mistral had dropped; outside, all was completely still, motionless against the oppressive sound of the cicadas' song. The Countess of Grignan took a few steps towards the secretaire and slipped the pages into a drawer with all the others, where they sat waiting to be collected into a book. I sat on the stoop of my building in the East Village, 342 East 9th Street, turning the postcard over and over in my fingers. There was a photo on one side, kisses on the other, and I was completely cheered up, because these kisses, this shower of kisses from my mother, came from a love that was completely sincere, without a shadow of narcissism or calculation. It was still early but it was already hot. The sky was hazy. The humidity on my skin felt like body lotion. I watched people beginning their day, walking towards the Astor Place subway (named, according to my Argentinian student – who chose to ignore the wealthy businessman and soldier John Jacob Astor – in homage to the musician Astor Piazzolla, who had spent his childhood a few streets away). Nowhere else, I thought to myself as I toyed with my postcard of Menton, do people walk so energetically, set off with such dynamism. They walk like that in the evening too, after work, though with a slightly more halting step, perhaps to chase away their exhaustion and the temptation to give up as night lifts the curtain on the second act and its promises of pleasure. I looked down at the postcard again, the turquoise of the sea, the lighter blue of the sky. Now I saw my mother, hurrying yet still light on her feet, with a step that made you want to look at her legs: the gait of a young girl. Her sandals showed off her tanned feet. "Hello!" she said when she saw me. And, beneath her restless feet, the blue – sky and sea – like a softly yielding carpet. She had written: "A thousand hugs, after a wonderful swim at Cap Martin. The water awaits you! Mama."

The water awaited me. The water was awaiting me here in Manhattan, too, the island where I had come to live for the spring, or maybe longer. It was very close. Late morning every day, after my language class at New York University, I took the A train to the beach. At Rockaway Park–Beach 116th Street everyone got off with an uncommon air of excitement for a subway terminus station. But long before the last stop it was apparent how different the travellers on this line were compared to the usual users of public transportation. They didn't have that sense of fatalism that characterizes the commuter. They had sunglasses and parasols, beach bags, cool boxes, sun hats and ghetto blasters. They jigged with impatient excitement. Puerto Ricans carrying picnic baskets danced on the spot. As soon as the train stopped at the water, everyone jostled everyone else out of the way to be the first to jump out onto the platform. Whoever was first off would be the first to get to the sea, the first to experience that dazzling instant when the sea's brilliance cancelled out its colour, and in the noon glare, splitting the burning rays, it felt like I was running and diving right into the sun.

I too carried a hat, sunglasses and beach bag, but I was the only one with my students' homework in my bag, resting on my towel that served as a cushion, alongside the wonderful little book selected for my course, Raymond Queneau's *Exercises in Style.* I walked past a group of people from the city who had escaped the suffocating shafts of streets trapped between the walls of skyscrapers and the steam vents that rise up out of the ground all over Manhattan, as if the city had been built on top of a volcano. I untied the waistband of my Indian cotton skirt and let it fall to my feet. I had my swimming costume on under my clothes. I kicked off my neat little heels, their soles slicked with tar: it was so hot that the tarmac on the streets was melting, shoes stuck and had to be peeled off the liquefying pavements. I was ready. I felt a head rush at this sudden reacquaintance with the sea air. The waves were long and gentle. They set my rhythm, the lazy, dreamy register of my swim. As I swam farther out and turned away from the flamboyant horizon to look towards where the dunes began, I remembered how I felt the first time I visited an Atlantic beach that spring. It was on Fire Island. After a journey by train and ferry, my friend and I walked along a sandy path that cut through the white dunes. I saw beach grass and pale pink flowers on a wild blackberry bush. The magic of their flushed petals took me right back to the beaches of my childhood. On Fire Island or walking along the sands at Cap Ferret – I was walking towards the same ocean. That day, in the bright light that haloed everything, I understood that I didn't have to return to Arcachon, everything became clear right there in those spangles of light and the beauty they radiated.

SEDUCTION

That September, after a considerable amount of prevarication, I left New York in the middle of an Indian summer to visit my mother on her flowery hillside. I was dreading it. Irritated as only she knew how to irritate me. On the plane I was filled with misgivings. We had only just taken off and I already wanted to back out of the trip. Through the cabin window I could almost make out each one of the solid buildings on Riverside Drive, along the Hudson River, their windows lit up, hinting at comfortable interiors, bourgeois anchorages, ordered lives (the opposite of the atmosphere of toughness and hardscrabble existence, the intensity of all the lost causes that emanated from the East Village and so fascinated me). They appeared and almost immediately disappeared from view, and, once the plane had gone beyond the coast and the white festoons of waves, I felt a moment of despondency. Why couldn't we just carry on, my mother and I, communicating by postcard? After all, we had at last found a satisfactory kind of exchange that managed to be both poetic and affectionate. But the flight had begun its soothing purr, and in the starry night sky that for the time being was my landscape, all my uncertainties and fears evaporated.

To my surprise, the youthful-looking woman who opened the door and took me in her arms with a little cry of joy was very much in keeping with the photographs and shorthand of her postcards and their garlands of kisses. In Arcachon I used to have the impression that day after day another woman had wormed her way inside her, was trying to take the place of the young girl setting foot on the beach for the first time, untying her espadrilles and looking at the sea, taking deep gulps of iodized air. For a long time I had practised, or at least tried to, a systematic indifference towards this "other" woman, the product of boredom and disappointment, a stranger who was ageing prematurely and who always seemed to be on the brink of a foul mood or a burst of anger – her way of showing us that the cycle of the seasons had long since stopped turning for her, that she had been left behind, crushed, under the low skies of an endless winter.

The radiant, elegant, youthful woman with wavy brown hair, no longer thin but still slim, who greeted me at Les Aloès was also a stranger to me – all the more so because the metamorphosis had been so swift and I had been unaware of it – but now she was a charming stranger. She wore gold hoops in her ears and a large brooch of yellow and purple gemstones pinned to her blouse. Mediterranean style suffused her whole person. She was beautiful and seductive. I was ready to let myself be seduced. I was not the only one.

Jackie had learnt to drive, discovered cinema, concerts, cocktails on a terrace overlooking the sea. Laughing, she let men flirt with her, but when she got home and the gentleman who had seemed so attractive earlier on in the evening (she didn't think twice about giving out her phone number) called, she pulled herself together and uttered the first excuse that popped into her head. She had no desire to marry again, absolutely not, *at any price*, and she wasn't really even looking to have an affair. She was afraid of the complications, intuiting the possibility of another kind of prison: after boredom, passion. I suspect she was also afraid – having only ever known her husband – of another man's body. She made excuses. As I sat there reading Colette or Dostoyevsky I could hear:

"I'm so sorry, but I'm not feeling terribly well today. I'm rather a fragile person, you know (*laughing*). Of course, yes, why not call me in a few days. It's quite true, I also felt there was something unique and mysterious between us." (*Hangs up.*)

"I'd love to, but I'm seeing my mother. Excuse me? Actually, she is not that old. She's moved down to the Côte d'Azur as well, of course I must spend time with her. Tomorrow? I'm afraid not. Tomorrow I have a meeting with my lawyer."

"You'd like to speak to who? No, I'm afraid you have the wrong number." (*Hanging up and looking at me as though summoning me as a witness to the folly of men.*)

There were times when no sooner had she put the phone down than she was filled with regret. What if he was the One? The man who was going to whisk her away to the Land of Happiness? An elemental rage rose in her. An urge to smash everything. She rang her mother, who had moved into an apartment at the foot of the hill. Her mother's lovely voice and laugh made her feel better. Together they mocked the rejected suitor. She checked herself in the mirror, touching up her lipstick and tousling her short curls. She poured herself a glass of the Cinzano Bianco she had bought in Ventimiglia (she loved her little Italian excursions) and went to sit on the balcony. In the balmy evening air, she would try to make out olive groves and meadows, terraced fields and pastureland on the mountain peaks inland. She even thought she could distinguish, high up, the white patches of sheep. Was the shepherd himself visible? Her eyesight wasn't sharp enough. Things like that, I said to her, depend on your inner disposition. If she kept a place for them in her thoughts, without obsessing over it – evidently it was a delicate balance – then everything was possible.

"I'm not asking that everything be possible. I'm just asking for love. That's not such a big ask, is it?"

Just then the telephone rang. "What a nice surprise! Of course I haven't forgotten you. I didn't call you back because I've had an awful lot on my plate lately. You men have no idea what it is like for a woman on her own." He had called at exactly the right moment. "Dancing, oh yes, I'd love that!" She did her make up in two minutes and rushed off to meet this stranger, this shepherd or Prince Charming. A businessman, as it turned out, overweight and unattractive, and on top of that a lousy dancer, who spent the entire evening talking about property deals. This one she was definitely not going to call back! There were others whom she might have liked more – whom she did like more – but she had discovered the superior pleasure of saying *no*.

She was becoming the queen of the disappointers. She found that toying with a man's desire is a thrill in itself, and always novel. It was not so much the scenario and the banality of the exchange of clichés, but a sort of fizz of excitement that suddenly aroused her, gave her a voracious appetite for nothing specific, a thrill when she caught sight of her reflection. During these encounters she felt the same euphoria that rises up with the first sip of alcohol. It took no more than a desiring glance to make her smoulder and in a split second become beautiful – hers was not a classic beauty, but the kind that thickens with something ineffable and can drive a man to folly. She became a devotee of the first date; she was such a romantic that it took no more than a few opening notes and she was floating on a pink cloud. It was wonderful – as long as it went no further. She became an artist of the brief encounter with no future. A stroll – quite dazzling – and then *pfff!* she was gone.

That she was looking for a man was obvious. That she was failing to do what was required to find one was clear. She began perceptibly modifying her behaviour. She started letting her admirers' hopes remain slightly open: just a little, but it changed everything. She no longer ended things immediately after the first meeting, and she stopped depending entirely on chance encounters. She registered with a marriage bureau in Menton. Then she decided she wanted to widen her sphere of activity: Nice, Cannes, even as far as Aix-en-Provence. This way, she said, with unwitting guile, I'll receive more serious propositions. She applied herself to the business of choosing photos and composing a description of herself. I helped her write her profile: sensitive, bohemian tastes – too much? – artistic, outgoing, cheerful, loves travelling. She didn't linger over what she was looking for, but she took great care over the wording of her most striking characteristics. She decided to describe herself as a dreamer, because she was terrified at the thought of falling back into the rut of conjugal routine.

Bourgeois-looking ladies (not to be confused with pimps) introduced her to men who were almost always either widowers or divorcés. Perhaps due to a failure of intuition by the matchmakers, Jackie was often introduced to teachers, which always proved disastrous; she was attracted by artists, with a preference for painters, of whom there were a great many living on the Côte d'Azur. She wanted to fall in love, and a few times she believed she had, but the minute the man – usually a grieving widower thrown off-kilter by the death of his wife – began to entertain the idea of marriage she would pull herself together. He had no idea how to live alone. He couldn't even make his own breakfast. He loved her. He wanted to marry her. She agonized, sometimes forgetting the first rule of flirting: keep desire burning and never end the affair definitively. Marriage was out of the question; not only because of her fear of being pigeonholed once again into the role of housewife, but also because she was afraid she would find herself looking after an ageing man who might at any moment become an invalid and transform her into a nurse. So yet again she would bring the fictional character of her mother into play, inventing an infinite series of illnesses with which she – in reality the very picture of health – was afflicted. She would cancel at the last minute, forget to return phone calls, fail to turn up to appointed rendezvous. And since, except when she was faced with a candid and urgent proposal of marriage, she was unable to tell black from white, she often found herself caught up in a whole series of affairs, pursued by a variety of lonesome gentlemen, who, to their great astonishment, and under the sway of her charm and vivacity, had discovered a renewed pleasure in existence. What she had longed for during her dark years of depression had come to pass: she was invited out to the theatre, restaurants, the casino. She began going to tea dances.

Flirting is a time-consuming business, but Jackie never let herself become totally absorbed by it. She kept most of the morning for swimming, and went back for a swim before dinner. She showed me her favourite bathing spots, the Ponchettes, the casino beach, which was an extension of the casino gardens, and Cap Martin, the most extraordinary place of all, where the sea was completely translucent, the liquid blue of a precious stone. Swimming there was pure joy, and as long as the sea was still infused with summer warmth there was no limit to how long one could stay in the water. I liked to explore the underwater life along the rocks, while she, ever faithful to her crawl, would swim out towards the open sea. Since there were no external markers for her to get her bearings, she invented her own way of measuring how far she swam, several lengths back and forth of exemplary regularity, with the metrical precision of laps completed in a swimming pool. We still couldn't (or wouldn't) swim together and even after our swim, lying in the sun to dry off, we each chose a spot hidden from the other among the spiny rocks that lined the cove.

She shared her beaches and outings with me, confided about her affairs. She was always delighted to go out, to break out of the false security of home. The only place she avoided, at the end of the promenade, was the Old Chateau cemetery. "Can't you suggest something more cheerful?" she would say. "Why don't we go and have a drink on the Place aux Herbes?" That was where Italians gathered to sing, their choruses mingling with the syrupy bitterness of Cinzano Bianco, Jackie humming along under her breath. Between that and a visit to the cemetery, her choice was clear. I didn't insist.

The Old Chateau cemetery, above the medieval part of town, was one of my favourite places to walk. I liked the climb up from the port, the cobbled steps, the esplanade in front of the Saint-Michel church, the gentle ascent to the top, from where, through the cypress trees, pink and white oleander flowers and rose bushes, there was a stunning view over Ventimiglia that opened up onto the Mediterranean. It made you believe in the unconcealed beauty of the world; all that was needed was to be present and to embrace it. I realized, as I wandered along the paths of the cemetery, that my mother was not the only one who wanted to drink from the well of forgetting. She was better prepared for it than other people, but it was the thing that motivated most of those who moved to the Côte d'Azur. Not having to think about the past any more, being blind to the future, or its absence. Sitting on a bench in the sun. Being hot. Being happy. Everything getting a little muddled in one's head, like the pretty tunes of the gondolier. And I too, wandering on this hill among the olive and cypress trees, statues of angels and busts where birds perched, sepia photographs, sumptuous chapels, broken gravestones covered with dead leaves and pine needles, jotting down in my notebook pious inscriptions and final farewells in English, German, Russian, the language of a young man or woman, a dead child, I was in the same peaceful thrall to the world's beauty. I visited the graves of John, eldest surviving son of John Sparks, England, Félicie, Prince Grégoire Volkonsky, Alexandrine, Dr Carl Schuez, gestorben zu Mentone am 21 März 1862, Susan Katharine, who fell asleep in Jesus, Étienne K., musician, Marie Léonie, Mother Saint François d'Assise, Sister Clémentine, Stefania, Archibald Mc Neil, died 31 March 1866, aged 25, Mabel, for ever with the Lord, Anna Macewicz born in Poland 18 April 1842 died in Menton on 14 October 1864, Alice Farquharson, who died on March 12, 1861, aged 12, Olga, who was dead, no longer living, she was dead, had lived so briefly before the book fell from her hands, no time to read anything… I walked, alone, gently anaesthetized by the litany of eternal regrets and the scent of flowers, until I found myself standing in front of the grave of Wanda, born in Berlin on 10 August 1851, died in Menton on 15 January 1912. Before she took the train back to Germany, her mother had placed on the partially shaded grave a ceramic bowl decorated with lemons, their unchanging yellow still gleaming in the sunlight. I often visited her grave, in a spirit of contemplation. It was just at that moment that three tourists appeared, a man and two women. The man was talking loudly, making jokes. One of the women was taking endless photographs. They walked past Wanda's grave without slowing down, didn't even glance at her beloved fruits, at the lemons that she herself had picked, that had made her so desperate to get well again, and I heard one of the women say loudly, to no one in particular: "It's like Arcachon, people used to come here to take the cure." "To be cured or to die," the man said, laughing.

His words wounded me like bullets. I ran down the steps, skipping over several at a time, down narrow alleyways and along shaded paths. The violence of these voices, the eruption of the word 'Arcachon' in a place where – according to the implicit, implacable diktat of my mother (she would have liked to have added to the deaths of people and the destruction of their personal effects the erasure of their names) – I had forced myself to forget it, caused my bubble to shatter. A diktat that I had had no problem obeying, for it is true that mourning cannot be shared, and this way each of us was left free to follow our own path.

During the days leading up to my departure, we continued to swim, walk, hang around the Place aux Herbes and make day trips to Italy. My mother had various romantic rendezvous. I watched her transformation with a mixture of curiosity and affection. I was no longer in the state of hostile tension that had characterized my adolescent years. I was no longer running away from her, afraid that she was going to infect me with her dark thoughts, but her way of wanting to be happy, with a man, by a man, through the eyes of her lover, through the reflection that he needed ceaselessly to offer her as a way of cajoling, reassuring, lulling her with endlessly repeated promises, kept me at a distance. She remained a stranger to me, a very special stranger, whose presence was coterminous with mine, whose moods, even though they were often incomprehensible, never left me unmoved. A very particular kind of stranger, who had become a sort of friend. In the evenings, I enjoyed walking with her along the Promenade du Soleil, or sitting on a swing seat, our feet only just touching the ground.

The morning I left, she stood by my side on the train platform. She seemed lost. She looked around her and said, her voice catching: "Menton is such a lonely place, just like everywhere else." I tried to console her. I promised her I would write more often, and call.

LONG-DISTANCE CALLS

I kept my promise. I no longer made do with postcards. Now I wrote on blue aerogram paper. But nothing I put down in either a letter or a card had any immediacy; every crisis and mood swing was expunged. Which meant that even though my letters were longer, they didn't move beyond the excited optimism of my early postcards; nor did my mother's, especially as she didn't bother to nourish them with extra details but simply filled them with even more symbols of her affection. Writing, like the little town of Menton, sheltered from the north wind, was an oasis of calm. Our telephone conversations wrecked this calm. They were rare, but they exposed me once again to my mother's volatile temperament, her abrupt swerves from misery to manic laughter, her disarming capacity to suddenly switch tone. As the months went by, a sense of disappointment began to dominate. After her initial excitement she was faced with the impression of a succession of failures and, more broadly, the dawning realization that there was nothing special about her situation. She told me anecdotes, or fragments of anecdotes, about efforts and attempts that ranged from funny to tragicomic to downright creepy, and I realized that there was an entire population of men and women – mostly women, like her – in search of happiness. Generally, they were no longer young, and had come to the Côte d'Azur in the hope of a new beginning, the desire for a new life, *vita nuova*, in the words of Dante (whom they had not read and probably would never read, for their dream of a rebirth did not include a literary curriculum). There were a lot of people just like her. The competition was intense. I thought about it as I walked towards Washington Square after an abortive telephone call with my mother. I had made the call from a telephone booth on Lafayette Street, against the deafening racket of buses, trucks, police sirens and ambulances. She somehow managed to force a fragile but insistent passage for her complaints through the hellish din. Exasperated, I had just threatened to hang up on her when we were cut off. I was hoping the musicians who played till the small hours, or the rebel poet who was always around proclaiming his rebellion at the top of his voice, were going to cheer me up. There was a telephone booth on every corner, but I couldn't face calling her back. I sat down on the edge of the fountain opposite Marble Arch and pictured Jackie, lost in the midst of a throng of elderly people. She was tossing her curly hair and waving a green silk scarf (which was how she identified herself when meeting up with a new man). She was smiling, and she looked so alone, so tiny, lost among so many other hopeful candidates for born-again love, that I too was overwhelmed by a sense of despair.

NEW LIFE

One morning I received a letter with a photograph of Jackie standing next to someone I didn't recognize: a tall, distinguished-looking, blond man in a white linen suit. And a hat. He looked considerably older than she was, but that didn't contradict the impression from the photo of a close bond between them. He was handsome and affluent-looking. He smiled like someone aware from a very young age that he was one of life's privileged, who, instead of experiencing this as a kind of superiority, had instead opted for happiness. One day Axel de S. decided that he was going to be an artist, so he left Sweden and followed in the footsteps of Matisse, Bonnard, Van Gogh and Picasso, to nourish his talent in the Provençal light. He lived in an old farmhouse above Cannes surrounded by his paintings and his companion of the moment, my mother, Jackie, whom he had baptized "Ella". Ella captivated him; she was the ideal woman he had been seeking his entire life via a series of unsatisfactory affairs. Ella had straight, light brown hair and wore loose, pastel-coloured clothes. He painted her from every possible angle. She – who had never been able to stand still and grew impatient after five minutes – could stay motionless for hours under his gaze. Ella was his Muse, his Beloved. He threw parties for her at the farmhouse. He wanted to show off his new love. Ella was a way of recapturing his youth with one last great love affair. When they weren't together he worked on minute details of his latest portrait of her, caressing her with the lightest of strokes. In the evening he drank whisky and wrote her poems.

Ella kept these poems wrapped up in a blouse tied with a green silk ribbon. She admired every word he wrote. The only thing she didn't like was his habit of cracking jokes. "You must never make a joke when you are about to make love," she would admonish him. She was no longer coy, distracted, mercurial or bad-tempered. Happiness stabilized her. She glowed. She never wore her "house face" any more.

He took her dancing at the fashionable nightclub the Siesta, just outside Cannes. During this magical time of perfect love, they were so impervious to exhaustion that dawn often took them by surprise; they dragged recliners down to the beach and sat facing the sea, eyes turned to watch the sunrise. Ella would go for a swim, her body tracing a wake in the glassy azure surface of the sea. He would watch her grow smaller as she swam towards the horizon, her presence no more than two fine sprays of foam produced by the regular motion of her arms and legs.

MY MOTHER IN THE STORM

I had been living in Paris for a while and Jackie had moved from Menton to Nice several years earlier. She didn't change coast this time. She simply moved from a small town to a larger one, from a small harbour to a larger one: from the Bay of Menton to the Bay of Angels. Over time she had forgotten Ella, her calm, her slow smiles and measured words, though she never forgot her lover, or his paintings of her as his beloved Muse. The walls of her apartment were covered with Axel's paintings though this was not an expression of mourning. She had never gone back on her practice of leaving the dead behind in their cemetery, of refusing to utter their names ever again and erasing from her memory all the places they had ever lived together. She continued to throw herself, free of any restraint, into all that the world had to offer. And indeed the world showed itself to be a generally amiable place. There were trysts, other lovers, and even if none stood comparison with her Swedish dreamboat, every relationship, as long as it lasted, was meaningful in some way. *Sport*, *Holidays*, *Joy*, *Sun*: she did not alter the motto inscribed by her father in his photograph album. She added other photos, lots of other photos of her in a bathing costume or a summer dress, laughing in the sunshine. Generally she liked to be set up with married men. Occasionally she would complain about the fact that they were married, but it was more for show, and she was much happier not to have to worry about the threat of a second marriage or, no less suffocating, of moving in with someone. "This way, you see, I keep hold of my freedom." We often talked about freedom, though without revealing very much; we didn't want to explore the question in any depth. Things actually changed very little between the two of us. Geographical distances were smaller and my visits more frequent, but the register of our conversations on the phone or in person remained as insubstantial and disjointed as it always had been. Before we had been able to depend on the brevity of a message on a postcard to keep us from arguing, or – and perhaps this was worse – to avoid exposing our insurmountable temperamental incompatibility, the painful evidence of our mutual incomprehension. The loneliness of a cry that is forever unheard.

We chattered in snippets, our shifts in tone and subject so frequent that if one were to try and illustrate our exchanges it would be with the literal image of wooden snippets – breaking sticks into small pieces, snapping them first into twigs and then matchsticks. And all it needed was a tiny spark to set the entire pile alight.

I no longer had to plan my journeys in advance, as when I lived in New York. Now I could improvise a visit at the last minute. It might be an overdose of winter or metro rides that never ended at the ocean. That was what decided me one day, though the weather forecast wasn't what I had hoped for. I arrived in the middle of an episode of "turbulence", to borrow a word from the vocabulary of air traffic. The plane had a bumpy landing at the airport by the sea, which, when you see it from the sky, looks like a slim, solid strip alongside the blue immensity of the ocean, a little beach specially laid out for aeroplanes to touch down and rise up like the seagulls that come and go on the shore. I love take-off – the steady unravelling of the clouds towards an azure blue that gradually appears and eventually triumphs, a triumph with notes of a Mozart overture. Landings fascinate me too. Specifically the moment when the pilot announces that "the plane has begun its descent", and the detail and relief of the landscape we are about to be set down in begin to appear. I have experienced better landings. The one that morning boded nothing good.

The plane descended through an interminable layer of cloud, not the lovely, airy, snowy, pearly-white clouds that delight the eye with their shifting architecture, the kind of clouds one would like to walk on; no, the clouds of this winter landing were dark, weirdly tinted with green, and dense, presaging storm and disaster. Down below, in the bay, where the clouds had completely extinguished the light, the mud-brown sea roiled with tree branches, pieces of wood, scraps of metal, even tattered old clothes and shoes; I couldn't help wondering from whose drowned bodies they had been torn. I took the bus from the airport that goes all the way along the Promenade des Anglais before turning at the Masséna Gardens and heading for the centre of town. It was almost empty, apart from a handful of tourists alarmed at arriving in such a storm and devastated at the thought that it had sucked their holiday plans into its chaotic wake. It didn't bode well if they were going to be shut up in their hotel room for several days... ("What does that mean, good weather wasn't included in the price?") The wind thrashed the palm trees and knocked over chairs; furious waves reared up so high they exploded, flooding the promenade. I was reminded of another dreadful storm, when a great deluge of water sprayed a mother and child walking on the Rauba Capeu promontory so heavily that a single jet had turned the baby's pram into a bath. The bus drove on through the torrential rain. Of course there was no one on the streets. Or so I thought, until I saw, walking in the opposite direction, frail, unsteady, but clearly very determined... my mother. I recognized her instantly. Bowed by the wind, she was zigzagging along the pavement to avoid the deep puddles. This didn't make her seem cautious. No one who saw her would have said that she looked as though she were thinking of giving up. She looked more like a stubborn fighter advancing towards an enemy infinitely stronger than she. The disproportion between the storm and the frail old lady that my mother had become was stark. It was a miracle she didn't slip and fall, or get blown over by the squall. She's gone mad! I thought to myself just as the bus was about to pass her, at the very moment when we were right alongside each other, I with the tourists safe and dry, she, surrendered to the wind, her face streaming, her scarf and hair completely soaked (her hair was no longer brown, still less the light Swedish brown it had been. It was white, thick and straight, styled in a cut that suited her fine features, their preserved beauty, which made me think of Italian renaissance portraits). The bus went by her very fast, but I caught a glimpse of her joyful expression, the radiance that is generated by touching the sublime. She might well have been lost, but I suddenly understood why, in response to my question, "What did you do today?" (a question whose robotic reflex and lack of imagination echoes the exact same question that our parents used to ask us when we were children, after we'd spent the day playing with friends), she would simply reply, "Nothing, I went for a walk" – how this *nothing*, far from being dismissive, expressed a sense of jubilation, her way of living the freedom of walking as an extraordinary experience. Fixing a destination, inventing some justification, diminishes, even cancels the pure experience of movement. My mother had never enjoyed grocery shopping. During the years when it was a household chore the very idea of it depressed her. Now that she lived alone, and could avoid the forced repetition, she had begun to find pleasure in it. Nonetheless, it was clear to the eyes of anyone who saw her battling the storm that this was no old lady out to do some shopping. I pictured some well-intentioned person trying to come to her aid and my mother's irritation, caught up in the giddiness of flight, her body having already formulated the fatal, delicious *yes* that sanctions its dissolution in water, wind and all the folly of our senses.

I returned home feeling happy for her, and with a newfound understanding of how little she had ever been moored to reason, and how I – like everyone else around her during all those years in Arcachon – had insisted on confining her to a role, and hated how badly she had handled it. This fugitive glimpse of her was an epiphany for me. For so many years I had been apparently close to my mother, in both physical proximity and enduring familiarity, but in reality I had always been separated from her by a screen as transparent as it was impassable; that day, when I saw her literally on the other side of the glass, I was suffused with understanding of the mysterious power of love. It was as if we were the same person. It no longer mattered which of us, she or I, in the blurry confusion of the torrential rain, was going to be borne away by the waves.

TUMBLEWEED

The next day I rang my mother's doorbell. She half opened the door. She wore her most welcoming expression.

"Hallo! How are you? You took quite a risk yesterday. It was a bit crazy to go out on the promenade in a storm like that."

"But you're the crazy one! What are you talking about?"

"It's true, I saw you. I was on the bus coming from the airport."

"Yesterday," she repeated, with a tiny note of uncertainty, then immediately regained her composure. "The weather was so filthy yesterday you wouldn't have let your dog out in it. I stayed quietly at home the whole day, it was lovely. I did some sewing."

It made me smile, the way she connected the words *lovely* and *sewing* in her lie. They had never gone together in our house. Back in the days of my great-grandmother Zélie, girls began learning to sew when they were very young. Perfection was making invisible stitches. That was the entire point: you had to sew so well, bent over your work for hours and hours, so that in the end there would be no trace of your labour. Impeccable hems stayed up as if by magic. Pleats arranged themselves. Little girls were taught sewing and needlepoint. Zélie was, apparently, very talented at embroidery, but she had failed to transmit her gift to any of her four daughters, Hélène, Henriette, Eugénie and Marguerite. Obediently, they all learnt to embroider well enough, but no better than that – well enough to put together a decent trousseau, judging by my grandmother's, whose embroidery was condensed down to her initials, E.F., in white silk, and a fuchsia-coloured carnation, long since faded. "A carnation for a poet," Eugénie used to say. "You see how I was already thinking of you," she would add in a whisper to Félix.

When Jackie was small she couldn't stay focused for five minutes on her embroidery ring, but she did learn to sew. For a long time she was the family seamstress. For her and for me. She excluded men's clothes, too complicated. She was good at skirts. I liked it when she made them wide and very gathered at the waist, so that when I spun around the skirt opened up into a circle. During these sewing afternoons – winter or rainy afternoons, never time stolen from being out of doors and specifically from swimming – the dining room table would be covered in fabric and paper patterns, and various materials to be turned into some kind of trimming. As much as I was excited at the thought of a new skirt I dreaded the trimmings… Jackie's mood was always poised somewhere between cheerful and irritable. At the first aggravation (pricking her finger, cutting something too close, or simply the amount of time it was taking) her cheer would mutate into irritation. Sewing, like patience, didn't take long to infuriate her. I would leave the room as quietly as I could the minute I heard her starting to fulminate, throwing scissors, cotton reels and thimbles into her sewing box and hastily folding pieces of fabric she'd finished tacking together. I would go back to my bedroom, book in hand, and get lost in a story, embark on an adventure. I'd be drifting down a river in Africa, anxiously wondering whether the repeated jolts against the bottom of the pirogue were caused by rocks, roots or crocodiles, when Jackie would open the door to warn me: "Don't go into the dining room barefoot, there are pins all over the floor."

My mother never completely gave up sewing, but she increasingly detached it from any notion of utility, indeed from any defined notion at all. Making clothes didn't interest her. It was too complicated and took too long. On the other hand, she loved modifying an existing garment.

This had begun originally with a sort of sacrilege, when a few weeks after my first communion she took my long white dress, unstitched the top of it and shortened the skirt to the length of a tennis skirt.

"Try it on. I can make it shorter if you like. It's not hemmed yet."

I felt it, when I moved, the metal of the pins against my thighs.

The tennis skirt fitted me perfectly and in the enthusiasm with which I ran and jumped to reach the ball it seemed to have preserved something of the mystical energy it held the day I climbed the steps up to the Basilica of Our Lady to take my first communion. The white fabric, fluttering on the Abatilles tennis court, was blessed. Puffed full of air, being worn for sport in no way detracted from its sanctity.

"What shall we do with the rest?" my mother wondered, scissors in hand. "A slip? No one wears them any more. Handkerchiefs? You really can't use your first communion dress to blow your nose." The religious nature of the original garment cramped her style somewhat. But it didn't take long for her to shake off her misgivings, and when she moved to Nice she began to indulge her inspiration freely. She would simultaneously take things apart and put them together, unstitching a sleeve to make a pocket, turning a woollen cape into a winter skirt, a summer dress into a cushion cover, a silk scarf into a lampshade, and trousers into shorts – all trousers, however craftily they tried to avoid their fate, ended up as shorts. Her apartment's small second bedroom was piled almost to the ceiling with clothes, the raw materials for her future creations. She sometimes worked there in the evening, listening to Barbara or Charles Aznavour, humming along as she unpicked the big gold buttons from a jacket to add to the collection she kept in a large metal box. She would pick them up in her hand and examine them one by one, as I used to do when I was little with my seashell collection, as children in Nice do with the stones they pick up on the beach. Sewing didn't get on her nerves because it was no longer a housewifely activity or a domestic obligation. And, according to her way of weighing up resignation and misery, the most unhappy women were without doubt the ones whom people said had every reason to be happy, and who, crushed by the weight of this illusory contentment, forced themselves to look as though they really were.

When she decided to hem something, she was absolutely painstaking, but according to criteria quite different from the limited objectives of a modest home seamstress. First she would choose a thimble – she had several, the most precious of which were silver and had belonged to her grandmother Zélie (thanks to their small size they had escaped the massive clear-out that preceded her departure from Arcachon) – and then a reel of cotton. Green, red or orange – something bright. She used *huge* stitches to hem, making them as visible as possible and contradicting centuries of female education, both religious and domestic, deliberately conceived to ensure female enslavement, to forbid girls from lifting their heads from their work for a second and thus potentially gaining access by chance or negligence to the heavily guarded masculine pursuit of Intelligence and Creation. She scattered bright blue, violet and deep pink all over her dresses and coats. Her cheerful lines had the conspicuousness of tacking stitches, without their provisional character. She would show me the garment and ask me what I thought. "It's pretty, no?"

My mother did not limit her sewing activities to fanciful cutting and cheeky tacking. She treasured another creative activity that was completely detached from any purpose or utility: she liked to assemble wool, shoelaces, cord, ribbon, trimming, silk threads, narrow bands of fabric, tinsel, military streamers, and so on, into a kind of ball that grew bigger with her finds; and as soon as it reached its perfect volume, like a snowball, she put it away, multi-coloured and dappled with glitter, on a shelf between a bunch of dried roses and a large red velvet heart. But while a snowball is compact and has no air in it, the strange balls confected by my mother were full of air. They held together but there was movement in their joins. Rather than balls that are modelled and compacted, virtual projectiles, they made me think of those assemblages of dried roots, stalks and dust that are blown by the wind along highways in Arizona, flying bushes that have something spectral about them: tumbleweed. Her muddled, multi-coloured balls had that same openness to possibility, and, because they were formed around a burning emotional core, they had a circular energy – though they stayed obediently still where their creator set them down.

With her ostentatious stitching the colour of fireworks, my mother was unconsciously avenging an age-old education in self-effacement: for stitching to be perfect it must be invisible... It wasn't an accident, I realized, as I thought of her exuberant, rebellious tacking and cutting, that sewing, *neat sewing*, *sewing to the point of exhaustion*, is one of the most common types of forced labour – torture – in women's prisons. I think of those women condemned day after day to sew and repair military uniforms for sixteen or seventeen hours without a break. I see their stiff necks, their aching backs, their bleeding fingers. Their worn-out, broken bodies. I recall a story told by a Russian female prisoner: a woman in the sewing workshop, on the verge of passing out, stopped sewing. The guard hit her and made her undress. The now naked prisoner was forced to continue working.

I told my mother this story. "How horrible," she said. "My God, such cruelty! Why are human beings so relentlessly keen on hurting one another?" But the idea that sewing, an activity that is largely female and domestic, should also be a punishment for prisoners seemed perfectly logical to her, given that to her home was merely another kind of prison.

Often when I left, as I was saying goodbye, or even as I was already going down the stairs, she would call after me: "Don't forget to bring me any clothes you have that need a tiny stitch or two."

Her offer of a "tiny stitch or two" made me smile. It was like hearing someone who strides everywhere suggesting that you join them in a procession of ants. Even as she grew older, she remained one of those people who only ever moves with great airborne strides, like tumbleweed. And the patterns she cut were getting shorter and shorter – she still wore very short skirts, preferring styles that didn't hinder her movements. Nothing tight or tailored. Espadrilles or ballet slippers. With her feathercut hair, short skirts and boyish T-shirts, there was nothing old-ladyish about her at all. While other people her age tend to become more insular and fearful, she welcomed unexpected encounters with strangers. She was interested in the philosophy of drifters, and liked nothing better than to sit after dinner beneath the white porticos of the Promenade des Anglais, chatting with strangers late into the night. She liked that best of all.

FORGETTING HOW TO SWIM

She had nothing to do during the day, but curiously she was finding more and more reasons not to swim. The first obstacle was her age-old enemy, the wind. On windy days, particularly during the mistral – unusual in the Bay of Angels, which was typically calm – she refused to swim, though she still took her swimming things in her bag and went down to the beach to look at the sea, standing there gazing out at its intense blue. Her desire to swim was as strong as ever, so she might decide to go to another, more sheltered, smaller bay, with a sandy beach: Villefranche-sur-Mer. She adored this place, and even on days when there were neither wind nor waves she sometimes took the train there. Afterwards she described these journeys to me as if they were real adventures, and indeed it wasn't nothing for a woman of eighty to walk to the station, take a crowded train, and then walk the considerable distance to her favourite beach, the furthest away and least crowded. There were often sailing boats with huge masts harboured in Villefranche Bay, and occasionally they lifted sail while she was swimming. She loved these coincidences, as though she were somehow part of the voyage, hoisting sail with the crew. She would come home elated from these expeditions, laughing in the face of fatigue. Swimming was the ultimate reward.

She had two quite different voices when she spoke on the phone: youthful and mellifluous on days when she swam, angry and upset on days when she could not. Days without swimming were pointless, barely worth living (and I knew by heart which of her faces corresponded to which of these very different voices). I tried to console her, to put it in perspective, though I didn't believe myself for a second, which she sensed. The injustice was absolute. And, alas, more and more frequent. Recently the excuses she had been giving me had begun to raise my suspicions. She hadn't swum today, she would tell me, because the weather was bad, or because ultimately, especially during the summer, the journey to Villefranche was so exhausting that it outweighed the benefits of swimming, however great they were. I would suggest that she didn't have to go so far: Neptune beach was inviting, and only ten minutes away. Sometimes she would tell me she didn't have the time, she was too busy, or even that she didn't like that beach. One day I suggested trying the neighbouring beach, below the Hotel Negresco, and offered to go with her. She seemed relieved, and held my arm hopefully as we walked together along the beach. We stripped down to our swimming costumes and I waited for her because there was a steep incline down to the water. But she didn't move. She stood watching some evening swimmers enjoying this extra dose of well-being before night fell. She stared at the perfect line of the horizon. Her sadness troubled me. She said: "If you can bear it, let's come back tomorrow, it's too steep for me here. I'll hurt myself." I protested that I was there to help her, it was still warm, what a wonderful month September had been. She withdrew into her distress, not wanting to admit to the nagging doubt that had begun to obsess her: what if she had forgotten how to swim?

RUNNING AWAY

Sometimes my mother would leave the house to go and buy something, but by the time she reached the shop she had forgotten what she had come for; or in the middle of a conversation, while you were answering a question, she would interrupt and ask the same question again. I would be talking to her and it was as if my words were just washing over her. Occasionally, instead of the usual sparkle in her hazel eyes, I glimpsed a shadow, a flash of fear. Nothing more. My mother had worked so hard to forget, had so actively *wanted* to forget, that now forgetting had become something external, a pathology, she was far ahead of people who weren't practised in it, who found themselves blindsided by their newfound forgetfulness. She was strangely at ease with the mysterious and active process that was erasing some of her existential data. At ease, not compliant. She sensed something going over her head, recognized that it was not the same as her willed amnesia of people and places that she erased from her world as bearers of bad omens and unpleasant, painful images – a successful entombment, where people, places, names were all to be buried beneath a layer of silence, as solid as concrete, never to re-emerge in a living space of conversation, laughter or tears, never to be alluded to even in passing, not even in a flash of sadness caught in someone's expression. My father's name did not have the remotest chance of breaking through the cordon of her lips, still less that of Arcachon.

When it came to this active desire to forget, any intervention by friends or relatives was unwelcome. The less anyone brought up taboo subjects the better. But in complete contrast, since a mechanism of forgetting had been set in motion that was out of her control, she had begun calling for help all the time. (I often came home to find a dozen messages on the answering machine, though this did not indicate any exponential increase in anxiety, for each succeeded the last as if all the previous ones had been forgotten.) Nonetheless, as soon as she sensed a serious effort to identify what was wrong, at the slightest attentive reaction, she hastily tried to cover her tracks, doing whatever she could to protect her solitude: she was fighting to preserve her independence, to save *her whole self* – complete with her long-standing, deliberate, carefully delineated memory blanks, and the fraying rest that was starting to recede.

Whenever I reminded her of something that she had said, that she now denied having said because she had forgotten having said it, she would retort, "How horrible, to remember everything like that."

The more improbable her wanderings and the more liable she was to lose her bearings in familiar streets, the more she was filled with plans to travel and supplement her regular rest cures with new, exotic and exciting destinations. They suited her taste for elaborate costume jewellery, coral necklaces, gilded belts, rings shaped like flowers... She was forever flicking through travel magazines, marking with a cross or circling the names and photographs of fancy hotels located in Ghanaian game reserves or the snowy mountain resorts of Sapporo. She loved these articles, extracted from an album of images of paradise. She particularly liked the Air France magazine, claiming that its dual language text let her practise her English, offering her the literal possibility of crossing a border. She planned what clothes to take, packing and repacking the contents of her suitcase, which she kept at the end of her bed, ready for her to leave at any moment, even in the middle of the night.

One day, just as we were taking an imaginary trip, mixing up my images of countries I had visited with hers taken from magazines and television programmes, entirely unconcerned with geographical verisimilitude, she handed me a piece of paper folded in four. On it I saw she had written, in thick black felt tip, "My absences". I felt my heart beat faster. I stared, dumbfounded, at the mysterious words. She smiled and said, “Read it, it’s the list of my next absences from Nice, with all the dates so that you don’t get confused about my plans.”

RETURN

It was May. Between the small railway stations from Bordeaux to Arcachon that dotted the flat, increasingly built-up landscape, poppies, daisies and hawthorn trees reminded me it was spring. It felt like a long time since I had seen it so vivid. So vivid and true. It was as if I were able to touch the very essence of spring. As if I were entering an environment with a well-maintained balance, where nature flourished freely, but with none of its menacing qualities. People, houses, allotments, fields of corn where the forest gave way to farmland: everything seemed to be based on the subtle interweaving of the outside – excessive, untameable – and the domestic, contained activity of tending a garden and making it bloom. It had been increasingly developed since I was last there, of course, but with sensitivity. The houses were low and modest. They didn't impose on their surroundings or block the view. They suggested simple, fleeting sketches of happiness. I had an urge to get off the train, pick a bunch of flowers and take a nap in the shade of the slim-pillared porch of one of these houses that were built to just the right proportions, I thought, my nose pressed against the window, for adults – whether young or beginning to stoop with age – and for even the smallest children and their pet dogs and cats, donkeys, goats, turtledoves... Sometimes I saw, in the shade of an oak tree, a table, some rattan chairs, a shawl draped over one of the chairs, a forgotten newspaper, and even, half-hidden under a porch, a vegetable patch with rows of lettuce and strawberries, and I thought I could make out sandy furrows from which poked tiny white flowers, and, alongside, caves and excavations being tirelessly dug and worked by hordes of ants. I imagined myself leaning over and watching them as the train continued its journey. Facture-Biganos, Le Teich, Gujan-Mestras... This flat landscape, this journey I had made so many times, these place names that I had heard so often, triggered in me an unexpected reaction. I don't know why these quite ordinary images, these humble glimpses of unexceptional daily life, fascinated me so much. Was it because they came out of nowhere, unheralded by any daydreams, and had never before aroused in me the slightest nostalgia? Probably. The fact that I had not once given them a single thought over all these years certainly conferred on them an element of surprise. But as the train left behind the villages and passed alongside the forest, and I found myself confronted by endless lines of pine trees (and my familiar, gnawing anxiety at the sight of them), my excitement subsided: I might have been fleetingly seduced by the bucolic, pastoral aspect of the region, but in fact the only thing I really loved was the coast. I didn't even think of it as a *region*, but as a *shore* – sand, sea and sky in perpetual interaction, infinite exchange. It was this fluidity that I loved, that made me feel I belonged there.

La Hume, La Teste... The train reached its destination: Arcachon. We were going no farther. I wheeled my suitcase in the direction of my hotel, the Grand Hotel Richelieu, by the bandstand on the square leading towards the jetty. Until recently I believed that the name of the hotel was a reference to Cardinal Richelieu, when in fact it refers to his great-nephew, Marshal Richelieu, an 18th-century grand duke, renowned from Versailles to Vienna for his loose living, decadent spending and wit, and known locally as governor of the old province around Bordeaux that used to be called Guyenne. I rather liked the idea of a hotel being named after a libertine. Before checking in I stopped at the Repetto, which had been one of my grandfather's favourite cafés. I was delighted to see that it was still there and carefully chose a place to sit from where I would have a blue glimpse of the sea. I have always preferred a view of the sea (a continuation of my obsession as a child with checking for a window or a skylight every time I entered a room, through which I could if necessary escape). It has always seemed so obvious to me that I have never been able to understand why anyone would prefer a view of dry land. And yet, I said to myself, thinking of François Mauriac, both have their fans, equally impassioned, who belong to two very different worlds, each blind to the respective charms of the other. Two kinds of people: farmers and foresters, sailors and fishermen; those who travel by land and those who travel by sea. I remembered Mauriac's impressions in his diary on his return to France in spring 1917. Judged too physically frail to fight (his formal discharge filled him with shame and a feeling of deep disgrace), he managed, after a year at the front as a nursing auxiliary, to be sent to Greece, to Salonika, as an ambulance driver. There he fell ill with malaria and was repatriated, exhausted and worn out. He returned to his native southwest France, initially to Arcachon, to convalesce – with his wife and her mother – from where he wrote: "Two weeks of convalescence in a house with Le Grix and her mother, as if we were on holiday. Storms, showers of warm rain, the forest bright with broom, nightingales and flowering acacia." He found his consolation in the forest, not the sea. This is what he said, burning with enthusiasm (and malarial fever), after they left Arcachon at the end of May to continue his convalescence at Malagar, the family estate: "Alone here with Mother. The air is scented with vanilla from the white carnations and orange from the philadelphus. Maybugs toppling heavily from the underside of the foliage. White butterflies trembling on the lawn [...]. The lowlands are buried beneath the haze of the setting sun, an unmoving sea that I prefer to the real sea. Waves of mountains that I prefer to real waves. I have never been happy living by the sea, that void of confusion and noise, vast yet formless, turbulent yet lifeless. Oh, unmoving waves of mountains that cradle in silence close to your heart all the joy and suffering of humankind that you nourish!"

The countryside, as secure, nourishing and reassuring as the presence of his mother... When he was young, the night before going back to school, before he left the family home in the Landes, he had a ritual of kissing the trunk of one of his beloved trees. Which makes me think of the fervour of my last late-summer swim, after which I will have to wait months before savouring the pleasure of the sea again. A last dip like a last kiss.

Before I went back to the hotel that evening – where I would carry on gazing out to sea – I took a walk along the jetty. I listened to the sound of the water lapping against the pillars and watched the slow-moving iridescence of the waves. It is true, the waves hold on to neither the joy nor the suffering of humankind, and it is precisely that – a memory that is not a memory, a lightness that is a kind of dispossession, the grace of being in the moment – that I want to keep with me everywhere I go.

I wandered around the town. I took taxis, buses and bicycles to get to Abatilles beach and the huge Dune du Pilat. I saw what had changed, and what had stayed the same. I compared. The other side of the bay was more developed and thus more brightly lit, and seemed closer than it used to. The Villa Pereire had been knocked down, the Mauresque casino burned to the ground, the market renovated, roads that used to be made of sand had been tarmacked, and when I went to find the rusty jetty, I found not so much as its shadow remaining. Now I understood the message that the jetty had tried so hard to convey to us, Lucile and me, and that we were too featherbrained and childish to hear – the existence of a third dimension: Time (its rust was proof). Had it still been standing I would have replied that of course I believe in Time, I am utterly fascinated by it, but that it, and its principle acolyte, the Past, only touch me when they offer me the possibility of living more deeply, more profoundly, more vibrantly in the present; if they make the glories of the one and only *now* shine more brightly.

I retraced the path from Summer Town to Autumn Town. I walked around Winter Town again. I crossed invisible borders and confused my seasons. I went to see the different houses I had lived in. They were all still standing and seemed to have been very little altered by their current occupants. The greenery in the gardens had grown and spread. Time benefits foliage. Félix and Eugénie's house on Avenue Régnault was now a holiday rental. I wrote down the phone number.

THE CHILDREN'S BEACH

The morning after the literary festival (the reason I had come back to Arcachon), I walked back to the beach where everyone had gathered the previous evening. The only thing left was a white tent that was about to be taken down. It was, coincidentally, the same beach that had once been Trimalco's domain, my childhood swimming club. An elderly couple walked past. The woman said to her husband:

"They were here, yesterday, the writers. Sitting with piles of their books at little tables."

"Each writer at his own table?"

"Yes, everyone at their own table. Individual tables. Like café tables, I suppose. Sitting like a row of onions, with their backs to the sea."

The man grunted. (I wondered if this was how he always talked to his wife.)

I pictured us, perched on our stools, our backs turned, as she said, to the sea, facing our potential readers as they arrived by land rather than water.

A wooden deck had been installed so that our feet, clad in city shoes, wouldn't sink into the sand. I glimpsed between the slats a category of sand that had not yet been identified: sand that was close but untouchable, momentarily unrecognizable, like some of the faces of my former schoolmates in the first flickering moments of surprise. This morning the sand had been uncovered again. I crouched down to touch it, letting it run through my fingers, feeling the silken rush of its flow.

It was spring sand, cool and slightly damp. The tide was out. I took off my shoes and walked down the beach to dip my toes in the water. The cold nipped my ankles. I let my feet get used to the shifting seabed, the water moving with the pressure of the current, the mystery of the single breath that animates the water and the sand flooding my body. I rolled up my trousers. I wanted to go in farther. The tide was coming in, and it seemed as if the sea was also coming to meet me. This was the beach where I used to do headstands, cartwheels and the splits, where I climbed ropes and went on the swing, giving myself the strongest push I could so that I felt as though the swing was propelling me into the sky and at the same time holding me safe with the crossbar. Then I stopped playing on the swing, and went back to playing games closer to the ground: I sculpted dolls out of sand, giving them seaweed for hair and shells for eyes. It was painstaking, slow work. In the evening, before I left, I painted a blush on their lips with a powder I had bought specially to colour them deep red. It was my way of saying "See you tomorrow." Sometimes, the following morning, when it was time for our gymnastics class by the sea (this time it was the teacher who stood with his back to the sea), to my great joy I would find them still intact, but that was rare. More often they had been damaged or even completely destroyed. It made me sad, but not for long, since I knew that later on in the afternoon I would start again. Each one, before I said goodbye, was given a name, a furtive but definitive baptism, the way it is said that some of Jesus's disciples, petitioned by tearful mothers, traced the names of their dead children on the sand, sprinkled them with a few drops of water and then wiped them away.

Thoroughly uninterested in the "sand that was close but untouchable", I hadn't realized that the children's beach and the writers' beach were one and the same, and that as soon as the writers' beach had been dismantled the children's beach had again taken over the entire stretch of shore.

I was sitting on the terrace of the Café de la Plage across the street, waiting for the seafood platter I had ordered to arrive, when I saw a little old lady, wearing an odd, crumpled lace dress. She was the same angry, disturbed woman who had come up to me the day before and told me, "I may be short and ugly but that doesn't mean I'm going to let anyone take advantage of me." She launched into a story about how she was being persecuted by her fat, foul-mouthed neighbour. He stole the dresses that she hung up to dry in the garden, and then dressed up in them to mock her. He was vulgar enough to taunt her while he was wearing her actual clothes, all torn and splitting at the seams. A nutcase, I thought to myself, and asked her to whom I should dedicate the book. In response, and with diabolical speed, she tore it from my hands, burst into laughter, and ran off as fast as her stocky legs could carry her.

I thought she was going to ignore me now; but instead she gave me a big smile and walked up to where I was sitting. I invited her to share my meal and she thanked me serenely. It was definitely the same woman, but now she was articulate, calm and friendly. I felt extraordinarily relieved, and even rather happy not only to have had the opportunity of this second meeting, but also at the possibility that I had received a sign from the Unknown Woman. Perhaps it is true, I thought to myself, that beggars and wanderers cross our paths only in order to test our ability to see in them – hard to discern in their visible destitution – the secret of a divine spirit. Perhaps it was her, the Princess of the Palace of the Sea, suffering and abused, regal and sovereign, enchained and free, strangely versatile, utterly elusive... I dreamt of her metamorphoses as I sipped my white wine and started on the seafood platter. I looked around for her, but couldn't see her. She had vanished. I trembled as I swallowed a voluptuous oyster, the cool, saline shock of it.

—

THE HOUSE AT THE FOOT OF THE DUNE

Jackie was sunbathing on the balcony, her skirt hitched halfway up her thighs, bare feet resting on her espadrilles. A wide-brimmed straw hat. She said to me, as she often did when I arrived:

"I need a map to show me the world. It's complicated to plan a trip without a map."

"You've got a map. Next time I'll bring you a globe."

"That's exactly what I need, a globe!"

I noticed that she had received the card I had sent her from Arcachon, an aerial view of the Banc d'Arguin, which was already pinned up above the telephone table alongside multiple views of New York, and also Djerba, the Pyrenees, Peru, Kathmandu, Amsterdam and Venice.

"And where have you just been?"

"Arcachon. I told you. And I wrote to you." I pointed to the postcard.

The name evoked no response. If there are degrees of forgetting, deeper or less deep zones where different memories are buried, then Arcachon, the promised sunshine of a seaside resort that had been gradually obscured by the ghosts of Winter Town, had been relegated to the very bottom. Her memories of Arcachon had been entirely erased, as though struck from the surface of the earth, and it was clear that no globe would bring them back to her.

I had a gift for her. A jade necklace, her favourite colour. She thought the pale pink pouch with a green ribbon tie was the present. I opened it for her and held a mirror up for her to see. She loved the necklace. She got up to fetch some wine glasses and gently stroked the wisteria as she went by.

Together we looked at a map. I pointed to Bordeaux, just above the tiny inlet of the bay. I told her stories about her life in the town under the sign of the seasons. I described all the different houses and it was precisely the one that I didn't mention, the one that for me didn't exist, the house in which she had spent her first summer there, that she suddenly remembered. There was a silence, then she said:

"I hope you remembered to go to the house at the foot of the dune?"

"It was the first thing I did. I watered the garden and aired the house."

"Did you sweep up the sand? You remember how it used to blow in under the door, settle on all the furniture, get between the floorboards, everywhere..."

"Of course, I swept up all the sand with the broom that you left in the hall."

She smiled at me and then, with that same light, twisting movement of the wrist that she used to have when she swam the crawl, she gently lifted the brim of her straw hat.

AVAILABLE AND COMING SOON FROM PUSHKIN PRESS

Pushkin Press was founded in 1997, and publishes novels, essays, memoirs, children's books—everything from timeless classics to the urgent and contemporary.

Our books represent exciting, high-quality writing from around the world: we publish some of the twentieth century's most widely acclaimed, brilliant authors such as Stefan Zweig, Yasushi Inoue, Teffi, Antal Szerb, Gerard Reve and Elsa Morante, as well as compelling and award-winning contemporary writers, including Dorthe Nors, Edith Pearlman, Perumal Murugan, Ayelet Gundar-Goshen and Chigozie Obioma.

Pushkin Press publishes the world's best stories, to be read and read again. To discover more, visit www.pushkinpress.com.

A WOMAN IN THE POLAR NIGHT
CHRISTIANE RITTER

MEMORIES OF LOW TIDE
CHANTAL THOMAS

MAZEL TOV
J.S. MARGOT

DAYS IN THE CAUCASUS
BANINE

THOSE WHO FORGET
GÉRALDINE SCHWARZ

YOUNG REMBRANDT
ONNO BLOM

THE WORLD OF YESTERDAY
STEFAN ZWEIG

NO PLACE TO LAY ONE'S HEAD
FRANÇOISE FRENKEL

DREAMERS
VOLKER WEIDERMANN

A CHILL IN THE AIR
IRIS ORIGO

RED LOVE
MAXIM LEO

A WORLD GONE MAD
ASTRID LINDGREN

ON THE END OF THE WORLD
JOSEPH ROTH

THE ALLURE OF CHANEL
PAUL MORAND

CLOSE TO THE MACHINE
ELLEN ULLMAN

SORROW OF THE EARTH
ERIC VUILLARD

A SORROW BEYOND DREAMS
PETER HANDKE

MEMORIES: FROM MOSCOW TO THE BLACK SEA
TEFFI

IN SEARCH OF LOST BOOKS
GIORGIO VAN STRATEN